QUICK HITS FOR ADJUNCT FACULTY AND LECTURERS

Quick Hits for Adjunct Faculty and Lecturers

SUCCESSFUL STRATEGIES BY AWARD-WINNING TEACHERS

Edited by
ROBIN K. MORGAN, KIMBERLY T. OLIVARES, and JON BECKER

Foreword by
BARBARA A. BICHELMEYER

Consulting Editor
ROBERT WOLTER

INDIANA UNIVERSITY PRESS
Bloomington and Indianapolis

This book is a publication of

Indiana University Press
Office of Scholarly Publishing
Herman B Wells Library 350
1320 East 10th Street
Bloomington, Indiana 47405 USA

iupress.indiana.edu

The paper used in this publication meets the minimum requirements of the American National Standard for Information Sciences—Permanence of Paper for Printed Library Materials, ANSI Z39.48–1992.

Manufactured in the United States of America

Library of Congress Cataloging-in-Publication Data

Quick hits for adjunct faculty and lecturers : successful strategies by award-winning teachers / edited by Robin K. Morgan, Kimberly T. Olivares, and Jon Becker ; foreword by Barbara A. Bichelmeyer ; consulting editor, Robert Wolter.
   pages cm
   Includes bibliographical references and index.
   ISBN 978-0-253-01834-2 (pb : alk. paper) — ISBN 978-0-253-01840-3 (eb) 1. College teaching—Handbooks, manuals, etc. 2. College teachers, Part-time—Handbooks, manuals, etc. I. Morgan, Robin K., 1961– II. Olivares, Kimberly T. III. Becker, Jon.
   LB2331.Q52 2015
   378.1'25—dc23
                                                    2015009092

1 2 3 4 5 20 19 18 17 16 15

CONTENTS

4 Managing the Classroom   61

5 Enhancing Professional Development   81

FOREWORD

The focus of this edition of *Quick Hits*, published by the Faculty Colloquium on Excellence in Teaching (FACET) at Indiana University, is teaching tips for adjunct faculty and lecturers. In this volume, the reader will find advice about how to use effective teaching strategies in order to improve and ensure student learning.

I find it a splendid irony that I'm addressing a foreword to *lecturers and adjunct faculty* for a publication that has as its goal the promotion of effective teaching and successful learning. As professionals dedicated to the teaching mission of higher education, the individuals who make up these two groups are keenly aware that their efforts to provide great instruction involve so much more than lecture, and that the lecture has never been the distinguishing feature of great instruction. The people who hold such titles also know well that great teaching cannot possibly be adjunct to the core purpose of a great university.

I understand the power of historical precedent; I know the titles of *lecturer and adjunct* have long held their place in the conventions of higher education, and perhaps at one point in history, such titles accurately reflected the work of these two groups. I am also aware that we are currently experiencing unprecedented changes in higher education due to the impact of forces such as shrinking revenues, massive and unsustainable growth of infrastructure, shifting demographics of the students we serve, new technologies for providing instruction and student services, and increasing calls for accountability. These forces are so profoundly changing expectations for higher education that we now find ourselves in the midst of a fundamental rethinking of the purposes, the operations, and the value propositions of our institutions.

In this shifting landscape, the one constant that has not changed, and that I predict will not change, is the hallmark of great instruction. Great teaching always has been, and always will be, highly engaging, extremely interactive, and deeply experiential. Great teaching always has been, and always will be, what brings students into our classrooms.

It is true that new technologies such as YouTube and Adobe Connect challenge us to consider what are the best means by which to deliver a lecture, while the "flipped classroom" challenges us to consider how we may better engage with our students. Great teachers recognize that new instructional technologies bring with them new affordances available for use. They understand that new technologies are neither inherently good nor bad in and of themselves; rather, they are good for some things and not so good for others, and it is the instructor's responsibility to learn how and when to best apply these tools in their classrooms.

The irony of all of this change is that, as we've seen the possibilities provided by new instructional technologies, they have served to clarify the fact that the authentic human presence provided by a great instructor is fundamentally critical to the success of our students, and the lifeblood of the institutional community. These truths are becoming more evident every day. The success of our lecturers and adjunct faculty is imperative to the achievement of the larger goals we have for our higher education institutions.

The purpose of this publication is to facilitate success for two groups of instructors who do not receive nearly the support or the recognition they deserve. So here's a figurative toast to the lecturers and adjunct faculty who serve our higher education institutions. We hope you find the articles in this publication helpful to your work. We wish you great success when working with your students, and we want you to know that we appreciate all you do for the greater good of higher education.

Respectfully,
Barbara A. Bichelmeyer, PhD
Professor of Instructional Systems Technology
Executive Associate Vice President, University Academic and Regional Affairs
Senior Director, Office of Online Education
Indiana University

WELCOME TO *QUICK HITS FOR ADJUNCT FACULTY AND LECTURERS*

The *Quick Hits* series of books were inspired by a gathering of FACET members who recognized the value of exchanging "tried and true" teaching tips. The idea of this group was to ask experienced and award-winning teachers to share what worked for them in the classroom. The initial volume, *Quick Hits*, has been followed by five subsequent publications, ranging from *More Quick Hits* to *Quick Hits for New Faculty* to *Quick Hits for Educating Citizens*, to *Quick Hits for Service-Learning* to *Quick Hits for Teaching with Technology*. Each of these volumes features techniques and strategies that have proven effective in the classroom; more recent volumes of *Quick Hits* have also focused on the scholarship underlying these tips and strategies.

Quick Hits for Adjunct Faculty and Lecturers is the most recent volume of this series and focuses on the needs of a burgeoning but greatly underserved population—nontenured faculty. Since 1995, FACET has sought to meet the needs of this population of educators through its Adjunct Faculty and Lecturers Conference (FALCON). Originally provided for adjunct faculty and lecturers of the many schools of Indiana University, the conference became a national conference in 2013 and welcomed its first international participant in 2014.

The theme of this volume is simply the needs of adjunct faculty and lecturers. For adjunct faculty, the reality of teaching at multiple campuses creates unique challenges. Both adjunct faculty and lecturers are confronted with situations not as frequently experienced by tenure-track faculty and receive less faculty development. Our chapters reflect this two-pronged approach. That is, providing faculty development—the same tips and strategies for enhancing student learning needed by all faculty—in the context of the day-to-day challenges confronting our adjunct faculty and lecturers.

Robin K. Morgan
University Director, Faculty Colloquium on Excellence in Teaching, Indiana University
Professor of Psychology, Indiana University Southeast

Kimberly T. Olivares
Assistant Director of FACET for Strategic Outreach, Indiana University

---

About FACET

The Faculty Colloquium on Excellence in Teaching (FACET) was established as an Indiana University Presidential Initiative in 1989 to promote and sustain teaching excellence. Today, FACET involves over 500 full-time faculty members, nominated and selected through an annual campus and statewide peer review process.

FACET is a community of faculty dedicated to and recognized for excellence in teaching and learning. FACET advocates pedagogical innovation, inspires growth and reflection, cultivates the Scholarship of Teaching and Learning and fosters personal renewal in the commitment to student learning.

INTRODUCTION

Education is ever evolving. The past 50 years have seen a dramatic change in higher education. The rapid growth and use of technology by both students and faculty (Kim & Bonk, 2006) has fueled much of this change and has drawn national attention as educators and researchers try to stay ahead of the steepening technological curve. Additionally, the increasing costs of higher education have impacted both the students in the classroom and the instructors who teach them (Lewin, 2008).

Another equally significant and dramatic change has received less publicity than these other higher-profile examples. In 1960, 75 percent of college instructors were full-time tenured or tenure-track professors; today only 27 percent are (Stainburn, 2009). Full-time lecturers and part-time adjunct faculty now teach the majority of classes at most colleges and universities. The reasons for this change are largely financial. As each state provides less funding for higher education, universities raise tuition and fees while attempting to cut costs (Waldron, 2013). Paying a lecturer or adjunct is significantly less expensive than paying for a full-time, tenure-track faculty member.

Who are full-time lecturers and part-time adjunct faculty? According to the most recent National Survey of Postsecondary Faculty (Monks, 2009), the majority of full-time lecturers and part-time adjunct faculty do not have a terminal degree (doctorate for most) in their area of specialization. Instead, most have completed their master's degree. As most universities require the terminal degree for employment in a full-time, tenure-track faculty position, these lecturers and part-time adjunct faculty are not eligible for tenure-track positions even when such positions become available.

Lecturers and adjunct faculty typically come to academia after having worked for many years in their area of specialization. Some of them have retired from their full-time careers and are supplementing their income. Others may still work at a full-time job in their area of specialization during the day and then teach a course (or multiple courses) at the university (or online) during the evening. The 'real world' experiences these teachers bring to the classroom are invaluable to the development of students who are preparing to leave the university and work in their chosen areas.

Because adjunct pay is particularly low (as little as $2000 for a semester-long course with no benefits), adjunct faculty often teach multiple classes at multiple universities. Lecturers are in a slightly better position, as they are often contracted to teach a full load of courses (typically four to five courses per semester) at a single university for a salary plus benefits.

These situational variables are important to understand. Given the realities of their lives, lecturers and adjunct faculty may have received little to no training in *how to teach* in their graduate programs or on their campuses. Although most universities now have centers dedicated to the improvement of teaching and learning, the majority of these centers focus their time and effort on full-time, tenure-track faculty. It isn't that lecturers and adjuncts are unwelcome. It's simply that meeting times are designed to more easily accommodate residential faculty. The issues addressed by these centers also tend to be more focused on residential faculty.

In recent years, awareness has increased that more attention needs to be directed to helping lecturers and adjunct faculty improve teaching and student learning. The *Quick Hits* series of books was designed to lessen the burden on the faculty member by providing a concise description of tested teaching experiences. The phrase 'Quick Hits' arose during the 1991 Indiana University Faculty Colloquium on Excellence of Teaching (FACET) retreat when several members offered engaging but quick strategies for involving students in learning. These ideas led to the publication of the first volume, *Quick Hits: Successful Strategies by Award Winning*

Teachers. Since then, five additional *Quick Hits* volumes have been published, each addressing contemporary challenges of teaching and learning. The early volumes were authored by members of FACET; subsequent volumes have been authored by a wider range of contributors and have become peer-reviewed publications.

The current volume, *Quick Hits for Adjunct Faculty and Lecturers*, addresses the unique challenges encountered by lecturers and adjunct faculty both inside and outside the classroom. While accessible for full-time faculty members as well, this volume has been written specifically with lecturers and adjunct faculty as its intended primary audience.

As in prior volumes of *Quick Hits*, the focus of each submission is on describing strategies that have proven to be successful. The strategies in this volume are organized into five chapters: *Balancing Competing Demands, Addressing Student Issues, Adopting Best Practices, Managing the Classroom,* and *Enhancing Professional Development.*

Balancing Competing Demands

Adjunct faculty and lecturers are similar to one another in many respects, but they also differ in terms of the demands placed upon them. Both adjunct faculty and lecturers may be expected to take on classes at the last minute, within days of the start of the semester, using texts that are not of their own choosing. Lecturers usually have more forewarning and may even have some choice in the classes they teach. However, lecturers may be in the position of teaching multiple sections of the same course, making it easier to plan for their courses. Adjunct faculty often have little say in what they are asked to teach. Their options are often "take it or leave it." They may teach multiple sections of the same course but at different universities, using different textbooks, and under different academic calendars and policies. *Balancing Competing Demands* offers strategies for maintaining organization across differing circumstances.

Addressing Student Issues

For adjunct faculty, finding space to meet with students may be difficult if no office space is assigned or if the only office space is shared with a cohort of adjuncts. For both adjunct faculty and lecturers, students may perceive that they are less credible than full-time residential faculty, increasing challenges to their authority both in the classroom and during conversations outside the classroom. Engaging students on a personal level and developing their confidence and understanding of the subject matter will help to eradicate these student misperceptions of the adjunct faculty and lecturer's classroom authority. *Addressing Student Issues* is critical to our success in the classroom. One student can control the teaching environment, for good or ill. Knowing how to manage these situations will make you a better instructor and will enhance the learning experience for all of our students.

Adopting Best Practices

Over the past few decades, increasing emphasis has been placed on the scholarship of teaching and learning, leading to the development of best practices in every discipline. For most full-time residential faculty, campus centers for teaching and learning have been successful in communicating some of these best practices through workshops and conferences. It is often difficult for lecturers (and particularly adjunct faculty) to attend such workshops and conferences due to their hectic teaching schedules. Asking these individuals to read the literature in teaching journals also poses a challenge due to time constraints. *Adopting Best Practices* offers short but effective, classroom-tested teaching methods to enhance the teaching experience.

Managing the Classroom

Students quickly differentiate between adjunct faculty, lecturer, and full-time residential faculty. As an undergraduate, we often joked about how long we were required to wait for a tardy faculty member. The higher the rank, the longer you waited; 5 minutes for an adjunct; 10 minutes for a lecturer; 15 minutes for an assistant professor; 20 minutes for an associate professor; and the entire class for a full professor. These differentiations are demonstrated in the respect shown by the students. In addition, lecturers and adjunct faculty may have received fewer opportunities to teach in graduate school and less training in how to manage a classroom. *Managing the Classroom* presents a variety of strategies for helping the classroom to run more smoothly, enhancing the learning environment, and increasing success for your students.

Enhancing Professional Development

University travel budgets rarely extend to funding adjunct faculty and lecturers' professional development opportunities. There are also few conferences geared toward this particular population. Although many lecturers and adjunct faculty may be content with their current level of employment at their university, many may wish to develop their research programs so that they might be considered for future full-time residential positions. At most universities, adjunct faculty may not even be eligible to apply for IRB approval for research studies. Learning how to navigate the university community may assist both adjunct faculty and lecturers in meeting these challenges. *Enhancing Professional Development* recognizes the importance for ALL teachers to be improving regularly, regardless of their rank, and offers suggestions for how to grow and develop as instructors.

References

Kim, K. J., & Bonk, C. J. (2006). The future of online teaching and learning in higher education: The survey says…. *Educause Quarterly, 4*, 22–30.

Lewin, T. (2008, December 3). College may become unaffordable for most in U.S. *The New York Times*. Retrieved from http://www.nytimes.com

Monks, J. (2009, July-August). Who are the part-time faculty? There's no such thing as a typical part-timer. *Academe, 95*(4). Retrieved from http://www.aaup.org/article/who-are-part-time-faculty#.UuEu1KX0BT4

Stainburn, S. (2010, January 3). The case of the vanishing full-time professor. *The New York Times*. Retrieved from http://www.nytimes.com

Waldron, T. (2013, January 23). State higher education funding has dropped 10 percent since the great recession. *Thinkprogress*. Retrieved from http://thinkprogress.org

BALANCING COMPETING DEMANDS

1

The shift from full-time to part-time faculty is dramatic. In 1969, tenured and tenure-track positions made up approximately 78.3 percent of the faculty, and non-tenure-track positions accounted for about 21.7 percent. By 2009, data from the National Center for Education Statistics's Integrated Postsecondary Education Data System show these proportions had nearly flipped; tenured and tenure-track faculty had declined to 33.5 percent of the professoriate and 66.5 percent of faculty were ineligible for tenure.

Of this 66.5 percent, 47.7 percent were part-time faculty. While the numbers of non-tenure-track faculty have grown the most at community colleges, they make up a large portion of the faculty at all institutional types (The Changing Academic Workforce, 2013).

These percentages are skewed even higher at the community college. More than 58% of the nation's community college courses are taught by adjunct faculty. In 2009, public two-year institutions hired 400,000 faculty members. Part-time instructors made up 70 percent of the new hires (Fain, 2014).

Given that the percent of part-time faculty continues to grow with no sign of slowing down, it is important that these valuable teachers be given tools to aid them in their teaching efforts.

Among the many challenges facing adjunct faculty today is the ability to balance the many demands pulling on them from all directions. The need to balance an ever-changing professional life with a personal life often means changing schedules on a semester to semester basis.

Factoring into a chaotic professional schedule are the unknown variables facing many adjunct faculty members every semester:
- "Will my class be canceled?"
- "Will I be switched to another course at the last moment?"
- "What if University A and University B offer me classes at the same time?"

Despite the fact that they are teaching a large percentage of courses at universities and community colleges across the country, adjuncts sit squarely at the bottom of the faculty "food chain" in the eyes of many administrators. They are slotted into the classes that are "left over" after the full-time faculty have had their say about what courses they want to teach. And if a full-time faculty member has a course canceled, the full-time faculty member will simply take a course that best fits his or her schedule away from an adjunct, usually without thought as to how it might affect the adjunct's schedule.

So how do part-time faculty members balance the many demands that compete for their time and attention? In this chapter, we have asked for best recommendations from faculty across the country to answer that very question. We hope that you find some help and some hope in the solutions offered here. And we welcome your feedback as we strive to meet the needs of adjunct faculty members across the country.

References

Fain, P. (2014). Low expectations, high stakes. Retrieved from: https://www.insidehighered.com/news/2014/04/07/part-time-professors-teach-most-community-college-students-report-finds

The Changing Academic Workforce (May/June, 2013). Retrieved from: http://agb.org/trusteeship/2013/5/changing-academic-workforce

JON BECKER
INDIANA UNIVERSITY NORTHWEST

SOME SEMI-USEFUL ADVICE FOR PART-TIME FACULTY

DEDE WOHLFARTH
SPALDING UNIVERSITY

I have taught full time for 15 years and have also taught overload classes as an adjunct in different university programs, including completely online, hybrid, and face-to-face classes. I have also helped hire and mentor new faculty, including part-time and full-time instructors. On my best days, I have figured out a few things that work in a classroom.

Keywords: Best Practices, Inspire Professional Development

Dear Adjunct Faculty Member,

This letter is what I wish I knew when I was you, simultaneously excited and petrified about teaching for the first time.

First of all, thank you for agreeing to teach a class! You may not always believe this, but we full-time faculty members are glad that you are here. This is true not only because we increasingly rely on you to run our universities (Flaherty, 2013), but because we need you to keep our classes "real." To share an embarrassing story: A group of full-time faculty members, including myself, worked for a year to create the perfect qualifying exam procedure. We were smugly proud of our final creation with its all-important rubric, minutely detailed operational definitions, and rigid grading criteria. It was a 40-page nirvana! The crème de le crème of exams! However, one wise adjunct faculty courageously questioned our final product as being complicated, esoteric, and useless. The truth of his words still echo verbatim: "This exam trains students to develop skills they will never use." After another brutal year of committee meetings, we finally realized that he was right and rewrote the entire exam to be more relevant.

Full-time faculty members are glad that you are here.

The point of this story is that we are highly invested in your success. So I offer some advice in hopes that you stick around and keep teaching:

- We hired you to teach because you are already are an expert in the content area. Don't doubt what you know. Instead, focus your energy on **learning how to teach** what you know. I recommend one great book to you, Daniel Willingham's "Why Students Don't Like School." Don't be daunted by the overwhelming number of books about teaching. Learning to teach is easier than learning everything about a subject, despite what us academicians believe. The hardest part of the journey is behind you.

- **Find a good mentor** who will not only share useful information about teaching, the university, and the students, but also where to park, how to use the university's likely idiosyncratic technology, where the important closet keys are, and what the code to the copy machine is.

- **Choose your textbook wisely**. Textbooks take more time to choose than you think and textbook choices are due earlier than you think, and divorcing a textbook is hard once you get wedded to it. Also: don't plan your syllabus our course around a book. Plan it around skills. Goals. Big dreams for students. ***What should they do or think differently after taking your fabulous class?***

- Please don't teach a class just once. Teaching a class for the first time is an inordinate amount of work. In proportional terms, prepping for a new class is like making \$.13 an hour. Teaching it for the second time is like making \$1.47 an hour. The third time you teach, it will feel closer to \$8 an hour and the fourth time you teach, you hit paydirt as you realize that \$20 an hour may actually be worth your time. My point is not that you can start phoning in your classes, but that **it gets much easier to teach each time**, so don't give up when it feels most hopeless.

- If possible, try to **get involved in department- and university-level service committees**. You will learn about the university's mission statement, strategic plan, and your department's goals for students and how to assess progress towards these goals. This information should help you immensely.

- Keep your life as simple as possible when designing and teaching a class by repeatedly asking only one mantra-like question: **"What will best help my students learn?"**

- **Don't rely on last year's syllabus** unless you are quite certain it is fabulous. The instructor who taught last year could have been the biggest idiot this side of Texas and the class the absolute nadir of learning.

- Relevant to student learning, we make some big assumptions as a field that better teaching leads to better learning. Theoretically, high levels of learning should define good teaching, but we have all had brilliant professors with fascinating stories from whom we learned … nothing. **Your teaching faultlessly is not as important as students' learning meaningfully**, so beware the false promises of being a "better teacher."

- I will summarize a zillion articles on the scholarship of teaching and learning in two words: **Active learning**. We learn by moving, doing, working, trying, and thinking; not by sitting, zoning out, watching PowerPoint slides, and listening. Try out these active learning ideas: Problem-based learning, case studies, group activities, field trips, and role playing. Messy, complicated real-world problems that scream for critical thinking, application, and integration.

- Share your stories from the field! You know the gritty reality of working in your chosen field, and students are hungry for your stories. Make stories relevant and connect them with key learning concepts. **We remember stories, not theories.** So, tell yours.

- **Every student is motivated to learn**. They just may not be motivated to learn your material. Don't believe me? Angry birds. Candy Crush Saga. Minecraft. We do like learning—we just like learning to be fun, interesting, relevant, and intrinsically rewarding. Ensure these adjectives describe your class.

- A special word **to those of you who are alumni**, such as I am: Reflect honestly on the pros and cons of being homegrown before you begin interacting with students. And even if you agree with a student who complains about the "Worst. Professor. Ever," and you know it is true, don't go there.

- I spent my entire first year of teaching praying in a bathroom before each class, some version of: "God, please don't let me look stupid." We are all afraid of failing, looking dumb, and being judged incompetent. Try to channel your nervous energy about failing into **modeling a commitment to lifelong learning for the students**. What a gift you will give them by doing so.

Sincerely,
DeDe Wohlfarth

References

Flaherty, C. (2013). Retrieved from: http://www.insidehighered.com/news/2013/01/09/adjunct-leaders-consider-strategies-force-change#sthash.aO7rwO8D.H9ATfJ8Q.dpbs

Willingham, D. (2009). *Why students don't like school*. Jossey-Bass: San Francisco.

NINE TIPS FOR MAINTAINING A WORK/LIFE BALANCE

MICHAEL J. POLITES
INDIANA UNIVERSITY PURDUE UNIVERSITY INDIANAPOLIS

Mike has taught Communication courses at IUPUI for ten years, the first year in the adjunct role, while also being a husband and a father of two young children. He has served as course director, academic advisor, search committee member, and conference planner as well as in other roles. His academic interests include retention efforts, engaging teaching techniques, and service-learning.

Keywords: Balance, Work/Life Balance, Tips and Suggestions

It is 10 o' clock at night. The kitchen is cleaned. The trash is out. The bills are paid. The house is quiet and everyone is asleep. It is time to begin grading those 25 papers you promised to your 9 a.m. class, right? There is only one problem. If you are like me, and I suspect many others, your brain does not typically function at its best at that hour, especially with any task that requires an element of critical thinking.

In this hurry, hurry, rush, rush world we often live in, balancing the demands of work and life can prove challenging, regardless of your academic role or whether you have a family at home or not. Even balancing the demands of teaching, research, service, and other work can be a struggle. It often leaves little to no time to take for ourselves. Further complicating things, many adjunct faculty members are teaching several classes at multiple colleges, and full-time and tenure-track faculty may be working toward promotion. Research by Kinman and Jones (2008) found that "Academics who reported more work-life conflict and perceived a greater discrepancy between their present and ideal levels of work-life integration tended to be less healthy, less satisfied with their jobs, and more likely to have seriously considered leaving academia. On the whole, academics who perceived more control over their work, more schedule flexibility and more support from their institutions had a better work-life balance."

Clearly this is a problem for many in the academy. The before mentioned challenges make that balance even tougher. So, what do we do about it? Here are some tips that have helped me over the years, and I hope that they will do the same for you.

1. Recognize that eventually it will all get done. Things may not get done when you want them to, but eventually, you will finish what truly needs to be finished.

2. Make a "to do" list and prioritize it. I use Microsoft Outlook's Task Manager to keep track of each class and what I still need to grade, plan, research, etc. I look at it first thing in the morning so I know what the day will bring.

3. Keep "regular" hours in your office and stay focused. I make it a goal to be in my office by 8:30 each morning and stay until 4:30 each afternoon. During that time, I challenge myself to stay focused because I know that if I don't, it's more work I will have to do at home, thereby taking time away from my family.

4. Be "present" when you are at home. There will always be more grading or work to do. Put down your smart phone. Close out your e-mail. Pay attention to your family. You will not regret it and they will appreciate it.

5. Discuss your job demands with your family. Let them know that you will occasionally need to bring work home with you. Come up with a compromise. For example, you get to grade papers for 90 minutes on a Sunday afternoon while your spouse takes the kids to the park, and when they return, you take the family out to dinner. The idea of being able to do work both at the office and at home is supported by Hill, Hawkins, Ferris and Weitman (2001) who write, "Employees with perceived flexibility in the timing and location of work can work longer hours before work-family balance becomes difficult."

6. Learn to say "no." A colleague I met at a conference once said he was "voluntold" to chair yet another committee, meaning that it was optional (in theory), but not really. To maintain a proper balance at work, try this response, "Thanks for the offer to serve, I would love to. However, I'm not able at this time due to some other responsibilities, but perhaps in the future." Consider too which opportunities will offer professional growth. This will also help in avoiding burnout.

7. Avoid being "on call" to your students 24/7. I let my students know that much like many of them, I have life priorities in addition to teaching. If I am grading papers late in the evening, I do not have my course management system open where I may be distracted by responding to a student e-mail that could probably wait; that is all done at the end of the work day (when possible).

8. Find your "Me Zone." Find that three-hour block that you work best. Do the most pressing tasks which require critical thinking and attention during that time, and save the less cognitively demanding tasks for other times.

9. Learn to deal with stress positively. When I am feeling overwhelmed and stressed, I resort to one of four things: quiet prayer, a box of candy, a video game, or exercise. Find what works best for you to "escape" and clear your mind.

I'm not trying to oversimplify this. Adjunct, full-time, and tenure-track faculty share some common tasks, but they also have some responsibilities that are very different and equally challenging in their own right. The committee work, grading, research, service, and other academic demands coming from seemingly every angle will always be there. I have learned to create the balance that I truly need in my life to be the best teacher, colleague, friend, husband, and parent that I can be. You can too!

References

Hill, E. J., Hawkins, A. J., Ferris, M., & Weitman, M. (2001). Finding an extra day a week: The positive influence of perceived job flexibility on work and family life balance. *Family Relations, 50*(1), 49–58. doi: 10.1111/j.1741-3729.2001.00049.x

Kinman, G., & Jones, F. (2008). A life beyond work? Job demands, work-life balance, and wellbeing in UK academics. *Journal of Human Behavior in the Social Environment, 17*(1–2), 41–60. doi: 0.1080/10911350802165478

I have learned to create the balance that I truly need in my life.

TIME TRAPS—HOW OFFICE INEFFICIENCY IS STEALING YOUR TIME

JON BECKER
INDIANA UNIVERSITY NORTHWEST

Jon Becker is a senior lecturer at Indiana University Northwest in the Department of Mathematics and Actuarial Science. He is also a former high school math teacher. Mr. Becker has been recognized for teaching excellence through his membership in the Faculty Colloquium on Excellence in Teaching (FACET) as well as numerous campus and system wide teaching awards. Jon devotes his professional service to developing resources for adjunct faculty and lecturers and serves as the chair for the planning of the annual FALCON event, a nationwide, professional teaching conference for adjunct faculty and lecturers.

Keywords: Balance, Efficiency, Time Traps, Organization

The pace of our world is accelerating. The ability to get information immediately has created a society that expects unreasonable control over our time. As a faculty member, if we do not seize control of our own schedule, our students, fellow faculty members, and administrators will seize control from us. Research by Klas and Hawkins (1997) on the causes of stress in classroom teachers and other professionals indicates that "...time and its effective management was the most significant stressor category for all groups."

The key to effective time management is to recognize what it is that robs us of our time. We all have 168 hours each week, but we marvel at those colleagues who are so productive while we struggle to get our tests graded and returned in a timely manner. Lecture preparation falls behind and we are unable to provide our best, most concise information to our students. Why?

In his book, *The Time Trap*, Alec Mackenzie (2009) offers a list of common "time traps" (based on survey data). When we recognize these time traps, we can develop a strategy that better prepares us to adopt and implement better time management tools.

Mackenzie's time traps can be grouped under two umbrellas: external traps and internal traps. External traps are often more difficult to control, because they are imposed upon us by others who are not aware of (or do not care about) our schedule. These traps include:

- Drop-in visitors
- Socializing
- Electronic interruptions
- Poorly run meetings

Internal traps are much more easily managed, as they are completely within our own control. Internal time traps include:

- Personal disorganization
- Procrastination
- Attempting too much
- Inability to say no

Effective management of these time traps will elevate productivity and increase our ability to teach and manage our classes well.

EXTERNAL TIME TRAPS

Drop-in visitors and socializing go hand-in-hand when it comes to stealing our time. As social beings, it is hard to tell someone who drops by unexpectedly that you can't take time to chat. Fear that we might appear rude yields control of our time to the unexpected visitor. Once they have control, it is extremely unlikely that they will leave until **they** have decided that the conversation has come to an end.

An effective tool for combatting the drop-in visitor is to immediately stand up as if you were about to leave the office. Having a "stand-up" conversation feels awkward, particularly to the drop-in visitor. This will naturally lead to a shorter conversation. If the discussion continues longer than you want it to, you can move toward the door, as if you were about to leave. Then you can go to the water fountain, the restroom, or anywhere else that will cut the conversation short. You can then return to your office as soon as it's "safe."

Another option is to set a time limit on your conversation. Quite often, the drop-in visitor will ask, "Hey, have you got a minute?" Instead of just saying yes, you can look at your watch and say, "You know what? I have just about one minute. What can I do for you?" If they are just looking for casual conversation, they will likely make a few niceties and then leave quickly. If they actually need to have a work-related conversation, you can offer to schedule at a time that is mutually convenient.

You can also use foreshadowing statements to let your visitor know that your time is limited. Statements like, "One more thing before we are done," or, "Before you go, let me ask you one last question," let the visitor know that the conversation is coming to a close.

Remember, your time is YOUR time. It should not be held hostage by unexpected visitors. These techniques may feel rude to you initially, but nothing in the work environment is ruder than having someone else control your time.

Electronic interruptions are easily managed external traps. Unfortunately, we have become programmed to respond any time that the phone rings or our computer chirps to tell us that we have new e-mail.

When we answer a phone call, we have no idea if the conversation will take one minute, ten minutes, or longer. Scheduling phone time and the use of caller ID are critical tools for managing telephone calls. Schedule a time, usually 30–45 minutes, when you will respond to all voicemail and e-mail communication. When the phone rings, you can quickly look at the caller ID to see if it's a phone call from your SMALL group of contacts from which you will receive a phone call at any time. For me, the only phone call I will take at any time is from my wife. All other callers will (hopefully) leave a message and I will call them back during my "electronic communication" time. If the caller does not leave a message, I will assume that they were just calling to chat, which would fall under the category of "drop-in visitors."

The lure of the electronic computer chirp is easily managed.

The lure of the electronic computer chirp is easily managed. Go into the settings for your e-mail server and disable the feature that makes a sound every time you get an e-mail. You will not be distracted by the sound, and you can check your e-mail at the same time that you are checking (and returning) voicemail messages.

Poorly run meetings are among the most frustrating time traps in an office setting. This is often because the person leading the meeting genuinely has no idea how to run an effective meeting. In the Chronicle of Higher Education, Gary A. Olson (2010) writes an excellent article on how to run meetings efficiently.

Before attending any meeting, request a copy of the meeting agenda, at least a day in advance. If the meeting facilitator can't provide a detailed agenda of objectives, then the meeting will likely waste a great deal of time. While objectives might be accomplished, it is likely that the time to productivity ratio will be way out of balance. Requesting an agenda will force the facilitator to think about what is to be accomplished and will provide a roadmap for the meeting.

Poor communication is often the result of poorly run meetings. At the end of every meeting, there should be an agenda item that specifies who is to complete what task, what is to be communicated to those who did not attend the meeting, and when each task is to be completed. These items should then be communicated through e-mail to everyone affected by the decisions made at the meeting, so that it is clear how each task is going to be completed.

INTERNAL TIME TRAPS
Personal disorganization is the key internal time trap that drives all of the others. When our workspaces and our schedules are disorganized, it makes it difficult to manage our time. There are two key tools in getting organized:

1. **Calendar/planner:** While elementary in concept, there are many instructors who live by the dates that they created on their syllabi at the beginning of the semester and do not centralize all of their information in one place. A good planning calendar will include an easy to use to-do list and is an essential tool in balancing the competing demands of an instructor's life. Whether that calendar is paper and pencil or electronic, keeping track of the wheres, whens, and hows of our schedule is critical to stress-free productivity—especially for faculty members who are teaching at multiple universities and on different days of the week.

To be effective, the calendar must offer yearly, monthly, weekly, and daily features that enable both long-term and short-term planning. Good planners will offer all of these options and are easily available at any office supply store. For those who prefer to go digital, there are a number of excellent apps (many of them free) that can be downloaded to your tablet device. I use the iCloud calendar on my iPad (it's free) but there are many other options available. Try several of them and find the one that works best for you.

(Don't forget to include class times and office hours for your students when building your calendar. Also, if you work at multiple universities, make sure to build in your transportation time when you plan.)

The second portion of your planner is the To-Do list. I currently use Wunderlist and have found it to be robust and flexible for my needs. Again, there are a variety of free options that you can try to find what works best for you. (There are also tutorials available on YouTube that will show you how to use these apps effectively.)

2. **Tickler file:** The second key tool to better organization is a folder system called a "Tickler" file—so named because it is designed to "tickle" our memory by sending ourselves a message in the future, making it easier to keep track of what needs to be done in a timely manner.

    I use a 45-hanging folder tickler file, and I have found this to be quite effective for my needs. The folders are organized as follows:
    - 31 files, labeled 1–31, are used for each day of the month;
    - 12 files, labeled January–December, are used for each month;
    - 2 files are labeled with the next two years on the calendar.

    When paperwork comes in, whether it is a set of tests to be graded or administered, a report that needs to be read and commented on, agendas for upcoming meetings, or any other piece of information, I file that paperwork in the folder on the date in the future when I will need it. If I do not need it until a few months down the road, I will put it in the file for the correct month. If it is a long term project that will not begin until next year, I put it into the folder for the appropriate year.

    Each morning when I come into the office, I pull out the tickler file for that date and remove all of the paperwork that has been filed for that date. Then I organize my daily "to-do" list, ranking each item in order of importance so that the most critical tasks are accomplished first.

    The use of these two tools has lowered my stress level and increased my productivity tremendously.

Procrastination is a result of ineffective time management. When we don't know where to begin, it is easier just to put out fires as they arise rather than work effectively and without stress.

Most people who procrastinate find that they are putting off the larger tasks in favor of completing lots of smaller, less important responsibilities. The key to avoiding procrastination goes back to your tickler file and daily planner.

Once you have the paperwork from today's tickler file, it is necessary to review and rank each item that needs to be done. Any item that absolutely MUST be done today should be assigned the letter "A." Any items that would be nice to get done today if at all possible should be assigned the letter "B." Any items that are not critical to your daily success should be assigned the letter "C."

Don't forget to include class times and office hours for your students when building your calendar.

• • • • • • • • • • • •

Once you have assigned all of your paperwork to a category, take all of the items in category "A" and rank them numerically, starting with 1, the absolutely most important task of your day. Then do the same for categories "B" and "C." After you have done this for a few days, you will find that this exercise should take you no more than 5–10 minutes, but it will save you a tremendous amount of time throughout your day. You have created a roadmap that will guide you effectively through your day. You will not procrastinate, because you will know what to do next.

Inability to say no and **attempting too much** go together when it comes to balancing the demands of university life, especially for those adjunct faculty members who may be teaching at multiple universities.

Each individual has to weigh carefully their circumstances when it comes to accepting (or turning down) opportunities that are presented to them. For example, if an adjunct is hoping to be considered for a possible full-time position that is opening up, then they are more likely to accept a request from their department to work on a committee or write a departmental exam.

Some individuals, regardless of their circumstances, just hate to let people down, so they won't say no to any requests, regardless of their time commitment in other areas of their lives. This is where a time management system comes in handy.

Too often, people do not think about what else is on their plates when they are asked to serve (This is a problem with which I have struggled for many years). By developing the discipline to say no, we maintain control over our schedule. At the very least, we can say, "Let me look at my schedule and get back to you with an answer tomorrow." This gives us the freedom to make a decision without the requesting individual standing over us and intimidating us into an immediate answer.

CONCLUSION

These are just a few of the time traps that conspire to steal your time in the workplace. As you work to get a better grip on your 168 hours each week, keep in mind that YOUR time is YOURS to manage. Never feel guilty when you need to turn down a request from a colleague or supervisor. Don't be embarrassed when you steer that drop-in visitor out of your office. As you accomplish more and more, you will experience the satisfaction of productivity levels that you didn't think possible. And you will wonder why you didn't start sooner.

References

Allen, D. (2001). *Getting things done*. New York: Penguin Books.

Klas, L., & Hawkins, F. (1997). Time management as a stressor for helping professionals: Implications for employment. *Journal of Employment Counseling, 34* (1), 2–6.

Mackenzie, A., & Nickerson, P. (2009). *The time trap: The classic book on time management*. New York: AMACOM Books.

Olson, G.A. (2010). How to run a meeting. *Chronicle of Higher Education*. Retreived from: http://chronicle.com /article/How-to-Run-a-Meeting/66237/

||||||||||||||||||||||||||||||||||||||||||||||||||||||||||||||||||||||||||||||||||||||||||||||||||||||||||||||||||||||||||||||||||||||||||||||||||||

COMPARTMENTALIZING, PRIORITIZING, PERSONALIZING: BALANCING COMPETING DEMANDS

JULIE SAAM
IU KOKOMO

Julie Saam has been involved in preparing Future Faculty Teaching Fellows to teach on any of the IU regional campuses and IUPUI. She has also worked with the IU Kokomo Center for Teaching and Learning to bring faculty development opportunities to all faculty at IU Kokomo including lecturers and adjunct faculty.

MARCIA DIXSON
IPFW FORT WAYNE

Marcia Dixson has worked with faculty development in many roles. In her role as director of the Basic Communication course for seven years she worked with graduate teaching assistants and adjuncts teaching over sixty sections of the basic course. She has published *Directing Associate Faculty: A Rich Resource for the Basic Course*, served as the director of the Center for the Enhancement of Teaching and Learning for three years, and has served as chair of the Department of Communication (which depends on over 25 adjunct faculty to offer its majors and minors) for the last seven years.

Keywords: Compartmentalize, Prioritize, Personalize

Framework

There is not enough time in the day! This is an oft-heard complaint in academia. Even with our best intentions, it seems impossible to accomplish all the various tasks required of teachers. Having read several self-help books and sought advice from other faculty, we have found two general approaches to balancing the demands on our time: compartmentalizing and prioritizing. However, we have realized that the most successful advice regarding how to balance competing demands is to personalize the approach and then personalize it again (things change over time). We will talk about each of these three ideas.

Monday	Tuesday	Wednesday	Thursday	Friday	Saturday	Sunday
Plan for classes	Committee work	Deliver classes	Grading	Catch up	Family	Family

	Monday	Tuesday	Wednesday	Thursday	Friday	Saturday	Sunday
Morning	Plan for classes	Committee work	Deliver classes	Grading	Community work	Family	Family
Afternoon	Deliver classes	Committee meetings	Plan for classes	Catch up	Grading	Family	Catch up

Figure 1.1. Examples of compartmentalizing by day or by the hour.

Making it Work

Compartmentalizing

Compartmentalizing is when you put your tasks into virtual compartments so your time with competing demands does not overlap. This allows you to focus much more effectively. This strategy can be accomplished by compartmentalizing by day or by the hour. Here are a few examples. (Figure 1.1)

The key to successful compartmentalization is not letting the compartments overlap. When Saturday arrives, you do not sneak in grading in the morning or afternoon, you spend time with your family or attending to your household. These activities need to "count" as important things accomplished. We understand circumstances arise where the schedule erupts but don't let that happen frequently. Eruptions should only be for emergencies.

Prioritization

Once you have your compartments filled, then the tasks within the compartments need to be prioritized. Brian Tracy (2007), in his book titled, *"Eat That Frog!"* explains that a sense of accomplishment and future motivation will increase when you complete a big, daunting task first. When you prioritize, move the daunting, time intensive, large tasks first in the schedule, followed by the little tasks. While it is tempting to cross off lots of little tasks to feel we have accomplished something, we are left with feeling overwhelmed because, after all that work, the daunting task still lies ahead. However, we gain an increased sense of accomplishment when we complete the daunting task first. This sense motivates us to complete the remaining tasks on the list. For example, when it is Thursday morning and you have 30 essays, 25 pop quizzes, and 10 journal entries to grade. Choose the group that you would find the most challenging, the most time consuming, the most daunting, and complete this task first. This also means you are tackling the "big" tasks when you are energetic and focused. While you may be able to grade the short pop quiz late in the afternoon, the essays might seem much more formidable after a full day of grading.

Personalization

We have learned through trial and error that any time management strategy requires personal reflection. It is a very personal decision what to compartmentalize when. I like grading first thing in the morning when my mind is fresh. Another faculty member would prefer to move all grading to the afternoon when he/she has time to reflect. I would choose the 30 essays as my daunting grading task and complete that first if following the Eat the Frog model. Another faculty member may choose the ten journal entries instead. Compartmentalizing and prioritizing are very personal decisions and responses to these decisions may change over time, may change from one semester to the next, and may change dependent upon the committee work or community work one is involved in at the time: thus, the need to personalize again. The key to remaining successful in balancing competing demands is to utilize the strategies that work, reevaluate the strategies from time to time, and reflect upon the strategies so they work for you. In personalizing priorities, it is also important to prioritize time for sleeping, eating healthy, and other activities that help you remain focused and energetic. In short, eat that frog and then eat something tastier or do something that helps you relax and reenergize: i.e., read a novel, watch football, or have a nice, relaxing dinner. You've earned it!

References

Tracy, B. (2007). *Eat that frog: 21 great ways to stop procrastinating and get more done in less time.* San Francisco: Berrett-Koehler Publishers, Inc.

RIGOR VERSUS REALITIES: THE CHALLENGE OF BALANCE IN THE 21ST-CENTURY CLASSROOM

MARY A. COOKSEY
INDIANA UNIVERSITY EAST

Mary (Ange) Cooksey has taught courses at Indiana University since 1986, first as an adjunct instructor, then as a senior lecturer. She has taught for several different regional campuses, and at numerous satellite locations across northeast Indiana.

Keywords: Rigor, Balance, Assignments

Framework

Recently, at a gathering of professional educators, the question was raised, "How can one attain rigor in a course without alienating the students?" In this microminute age of 'Get it done quick' and 'being prepared' means doing it an hour before the deadline, students have proven to have little patience for complicated tasks or complex homework assignments. And sometimes with good reason. Their lives are busy. They juggle numerous demands and obligations, causing constant and fierce competition for their time. When it comes to their homework, if they cannot 'Google' for a fast answer or find one in Wikipedia, they may lay the assignment aside or fail to invest the time needed to accomplish its ideal learning outcomes or objectives. However, some skill sets and knowledge bases require more than a 'rough and ready' approach to gain command of them and acquire expertise, and some more advanced habits of mind require more elegant exercises in order to develop appropriately. So how does today's educator respond to this need to integrate rigor into students' coursework, while at the same time remaining sympathetic and sensitive to the realities faced by overwhelmed, overworked, time-strapped students?

In order to meet the challenge of balance between rigor and realities in the classroom, today's educators might be well served in following 3 Rs: Rationale, Reason, and Reusability. Each will be defined and discussed in turn, with an example presented to guide future and individualized application in practice.

Making It Work

RATIONALE

The first step in finding a balance between rigor and realities in the classroom is to proceed from a solid rationale for the rigor being integrated into the coursework. Delineating specific learning objectives, and developing precise, rigorous activities in which to engage students will encourage the attainment of desired outcomes. Match rigor in task to desired rigor in skill. Example: If the specific, desired learning outcome in the study of symbolic Logic is students' development of skill in recognizing the difference between a fallacy and a defensible argument, assignment of problems wherein the application of that very skill in intellectual discernment is required and becomes the assignment of choice—no matter how difficult and time consuming this homework might seem. The rigor inherent in problem solving matches the rigor displayed by deliberate deconstruction and explication of arguments, thus established a solid rationale for the integration of the rigor in the coursework for students.

REASON

In the balance between rigor and realities, the role of reason is to act as the conduit through which the pedagogical rationale may flow more freely to the student. The word 'reason' is being used in two ways here: one, an extension of the rationale for the rigor in the form of the answer to the 'why' for the integration in the first place, and two, an intellectual application of choice in method of presentation of material and assignment of form in task independent of pedagogical rationale for the integration of rigor. Example: Returning to the study of symbolic Logic, the preferred mode of presentation and assignment of form in task is mathematical. Laws and theorems are presented in proof as linear expressions, with symbols marking entities bounded by operations expressed by method of movement from one line to another, ultimately leading to a solution or conclusion. Logic is the ideological 'toolkit' of Philosophy, operationalized through mathematical language, so mathematical language is the method through which to best present discipline content and by which to assign course tasks to encourage development of student skill through assignment of like homework. Again, as with rationale for rigor, reason for rigor must meet the challenge of balance between that inherent in the skill to be acquired and that inherent in the task assigned through which to develop that skill. If the balance between these two obtain, the reason for the integration of rigor into coursework will be more readily observable, understandable and accepted by students.

REUSABILITY

Paramount in sustaining the balance between rigor and realities in the classroom is to integrate that which has the broadest application and the longest shelf life for the student. Critical thinking, assimilation of diverse information, and creative problem solving are highly desirable skills for nearly every profession in the 21st century. Integration of rigor in assignments for students may in some way, shape, or form, encourage the development of one or more of these skills. Example: The study of symbolic Logic automatically lends itself to the development of skill in critical thinking, assimilation of diverse information, and creative problem solving. But what about a less obvious example like that of the desire to integrate course assignments with rigor in Ethics class in order to encourage the development of objective explication of emotionally charged moral issues? The explication of case studies would require the application of such idea architecture —and no matter how difficult or time consuming, the learning objective or outcome would be the development of objective explication of emotionally charged moral issues, a skill students could apply over and over again in their personal and professional lives. This high degree of reusability would sustain the assignment or activity in the face of scrutiny brought on by the overscheduled, overextended 21st-century student. The reusability would justify the integration of the rigor.

Future Implications

In working to discover and maintain the balance between rigor and realities in the 21st-century classroom, educators must be willing to develop a pedagogical approach wherein the 3 Rs are frontloaded into the course, and assessment is conducted to measure for the attainment of learning outcomes. Whether through the administration of a pre-test and post-test in a course like Logic, or the assignment of a case study-based, reflective writing in a class like Ethics, using a 'tried and true' assessment tool to measure attainment of learning objectives will provide feedback for efficient and effective course refinement.

REDUCE TIME SPENT GRADING: USE RUBRICS!

ROBIN K. MORGAN
INDIANA UNIVERSITY SOUTHEAST

Robin is currently a professor of psychology and serves as the university director of the Faculty Colloquium on Excellence in Teaching. As a graduate student, she also taught as an adjunct faculty member at a community college.

Keywords: Time Management, Rubric, Grading

A colleague of mine complains every semester about how long he spends grading student research papers. First, he reads each paper. He then goes back and makes corrections for spelling, typographical, and grammatical errors. After this, he reviews each paper for organization and flow. Finally, he reads each paper for content and support for arguments. All in all, he spends approximately two hours on each student's paper.

When he asks me how long I spend on grading, I tell him about 10 minutes per student paper. How can I do this? (No, I don't randomly assign grades!) I have finally discovered rubrics.

A rubric is a scoring tool that explicitly represents my expectations for students on an assignment. As the professor, I create the rubric based on what I believe are the important component parts of the assignment. These component parts are based on my stated student learning objectives (outcomes). Each component is further explicitly described. That is, a student will know by looking at the rubric how many points are allocated for each component and the breakdown of points within that component. There are numerous examples of rubrics online and clear cut procedures for developing your own rubrics (e.g., http://teaching.berkeley.edu/rubrics).

Rubrics provide many advantages—to the instructor and to the student. For the student, a rubric provides clear guidelines on what their instructor expects. With a rubric, the student is also provided specific and clear feedback on their work, allowing them to improve. As an instructor. The process of creating a rubric allows me to reflect on the purpose of the assignment, what I value in the assignment, and how the assignment fits into my course learning outcomes. Finally, using the rubric significantly decreases the time I spend grading. Instead of writing comments or correcting papers, I simply read the paper, marking the rubric as I read. When I finish reading, the rubric is completed and the paper is graded. With many learning management systems, rubrics can be added to the system and points are totaled.

Overall, rubrics significantly reduce the time I spend grading as well as helping students understand my expectations before they begin writing. Of course, I spend extra time developing my rubrics but this time pays for itself in the grading process.

SECRET AGENT

KAREN JOHNSON

Karen juggles life and working at seven universities as an adjunct.

Keywords: Balance, Multiple Universities, Online Teaching

I am a secret agent! Actually, I am an adjunct professor juggling seven (yes … 7) adjunct positions while raising a family and participating in several volunteer positions. Why do I feel like a secret agent? Teaching at seven institutes in order to maintain what I call a "healthy" income requires me to be a little under cover. Would all seven institutes hire me if they knew? Why not? I work hard. I am dedicated and I am able to keep up with the requirements for each school so why do I worry and how do I do it? Why do I sometimes feel like I am an undercover agent? Adjuncts are part time so my concern is that the institute I work for may wonder if I am committed to their goals and missions if I work for another institute. The answer is Yes! Does commitment mean I cannot work for someone else? The truth is NO… so with this letter I am coming out and letting everyone know that I am a responsible, dedicated, and hardworking adjunct instructor who is committed to excellence while working for more than one institute.

How do I keep it all together? I am a project manager by trade so I definitely understand the need for process control, change control, risk management, and time management. For starters, I have a weekly calendar that contains all of the requirements for each school and I add in additional comments and appointments as needed. I also make good use of my iPhone calendar reminders. Yes, I have at least 40 alarms hard coded to remind me of my weekly schedule. You know what they say… off the brain and on to the paper makes for less stress. I am living proof. From the time my feet hit the floor alarms go off reminding me of my day. It works great! My kids (and grandkids) get to where they need to be … on time. I am able to manage my day effectively while taking care of home, elderly parents and the daily grind of this beautiful life while working a total of eight jobs! Eight?

I also still find time to do my volunteer work with several organizations. My husband calls them my "Free" jobs! He always asks me… "How much are you getting paid for that job…? Oh, that's right the pay is the same … FREE!"

Don't forget my family which includes six children and 6 grandchildren. As a side note, some of my children and grandchildren are the same age!!!! I call this a "free" job but this is the free job that is not a job at all. It is what makes me whole! Let's face it … cooking, cleaning, and managing a household sometimes feels like work, but if you are like me you love every minute of it.

On top of all of this … I substitute teach at the grade level in my spare time? Spare time, I actually have a lot more in the sense that four of my schools are online schools. Now don't get me wrong—anyone who has taken an online class knows the demands are tremendous and most classes require a lot of writing which is why I am a great reader. In fact, I completed my undergrad, two master's degrees, and a PhD all online! Teaching from home means I cut down significantly on commuting time. Until three years ago I worked in Corporate America. I drove at least 2 hours each day round trip. With online, no more traffic!!! I also don't have to work 8–10 hours each day. Instead I have flexible hours of which I try to set aside at least one day a week where I don't do any school work. This is officially called my SANITY day. Guess what… today is sanity day and my most important "free" job is calling me … My kids and family! Gotta go!

BALANCING COMPETING DEMANDS WHEN WORKING AS AN ADJUNCT

LINDA CHRISTIANSEN
INDIANA UNIVERSITY SOUTHEAST

Professor Christiansen has taught as an adjunct at four universities within a five-year period and served as a lecturer for five years (first as visiting and then permanent) before moving into a tenure-track position. She is now a full professor of Business, teaching business law, business ethics, and accounting. For the past six years, she has hired, supervised, and mentored the adjunct faculty in Accounting and Business Law.

Keywords: Balance, Time Management

Most adjuncts must balance a variety of responsibilities, including adjunct classes at more than one school or in combination with full-time jobs.

Introduction

Time is short when working another job or teaching at more than one school, and flexibility is limited. A few key investments will make balancing your jobs and life easier both in the short term and in the long term; they will benefit your students and could even lead to a full-time job, if that is what you desire. (See article entitled "Converting an Adjunct Position to Lecturer or Tenure-Track Position" in this book.) I have used all of the ideas offered here; many were valuable to me when I was an adjunct, and I have adopted several as they became available as a result of developing technology.

Read the Faculty Manual/Handbook

One of the first things I did when I became an adjunct was to read the Faculty Manual for guidelines concerning what is require or allowed and what is not allowed. It served me well in numerous ways as an adjunct and continues to benefit me to this day.

Be Organized and Proactive

When working in more than one place, you simply cannot leave things to the last minute. Plan to prepare well in advance and also to review within 24 hours of class. It is very important to have studied and mastered the material in-depth in advance in order to be prepared and to formulate assignments in case of busyness with other areas of your life. It is also important to review so as to be fresh with the material you will be presenting on any given day.

Write and print/post assignments, tests, and quizzes early. While it can be tempting and sometimes necessary to prepare at the last minute, too many things can go wrong. A broken copier or a long printing line right before class time is not uncommon. Adjuncts face traffic and parking issues going from job to job, which add uncertainty to arrival times. Prepare and print as early as possible.

University Resources

Sometimes it can feel like you have to create the course yourself. That is not true. Ask faculty or administrators in your discipline if they will share syllabi, assignment ideas, tests, publisher resources, and other course materials. With their assistance, you do not have to 'reinvent the wheel' and can benefit from work that has already been done.

Inquire about and investigate university resources available to you and to students. Many schools have teaching and learning offices willing to offer assistance and programs to adjunct faculty. Likewise, discover what university resources are available to students (e.g., writing and math labs, library and research assistance, career centers, or counseling) so that you can recommend and include information on your syllabus, as applicable.

Technology

Technology is an excellent resource to leverage your time and efforts. This is an area with which colleagues and the teaching and learning center can help you discover, learn, and manage what is offered at your university.

Make some office hours virtual, if possible. You can use chat rooms or online meeting software to facilitate online office hours. There is a good chance that many of your students are as pressed for time as you are or have conflicts with scheduled office hours. Many students need or would like the flexibility virtual office hours provide. Another idea is to have students respond to the questions of other students in a blog or discussion forum format. They will learn more and deeper by explaining the material to each other.

Discussion forums are very valuable ways to provide opportunities every student to take part in discussion and analysis for a hybrid or online format, or for a time when you cannot hold class.

You can also use technology to offer additional feedback to students. If you require multiple drafts of an assignment or a series of similar assignments, you can extend the benefits of your grading one or more drafts in the series by also having students give feedback to each other on one or more of the drafts or assignments. Students can learn from reading and assessing another's strengths and weaknesses. Provide a grading rubric as a structure for the student feedback. Online group blogs and discussion forums are good tools for this exercise.

Conflicts with Other Employment

Adjuncts who teach while working in their discipline they are teaching can add valuable real-world experience and examples to the class, but doing both also presents challenging demands (e.g., travel or other reasons to miss class) and less flexibility in general.

Is a hybrid/blended or online format an option, or is it even welcomed and encouraged at your university? Online teaching does not decrease the amount of work and responsibilities, but it adds flexibility as to the timing to accomplishing those duties.

If you happen to travel for work, make arrangements with your school or colleagues to find the best solution. Perhaps you can schedule a project or exam, or develop an online assignment using the university course management system. Ask if a colleague can proctor an exam or teach a class session. You might be able to schedule a special speaker for that day.

Student Issues

If you have any issues with students, always check with your supervisor or faculty in the area. Never hesitate to ask how you should handle a situation. I have told every adjunct I hired and mentored to do this, and as a result, we avoided potentially problematic situations. This allows the full-time employees to handle the situation and make the hard decisions and also provides an opportunity to build relationships and trust with colleagues.

Conclusion

With some diligence, focus, and tried-and-true ideas, balancing the competing demands of working as an adjunct along with other jobs and life obligations can be manageable. If you have a desire to teach, these ideas will help you manage the details and allow you to enjoy the goal: educating students.

With some diligence, focus, and tried-and-true ideas,
balancing the competing demands of working as an adjunct along
with other jobs and life obligations
can be manageable.

Addressing Student Issues

2

We live in a rapidly changing world. As we push through the information age into what some label the "creative age," we must examine our teaching approaches and continually create a multifaceted approach to teaching and learning. In the technologically saturated world in which we operate, educators need to strategize and consider nontraditional ways to reach their students. Gone are the days of a one sided-lecture in which students sit passively at their desks, writing all hour, waiting for the droning to end. While the issues students face today are similar to those experienced for decades, the ways in which we respond to these issues must evolve with the movement of time and technology. Today, teaching and learning are enhanced and burdened with instant access to a plethora of information, some good, and some of little value. Consequently, educators must take an active approach to student engagement and empowerment in the classroom to facilitate student comprehension, interaction, and synthesis of relevant course content and concepts. We need to empower our students to think critically and discern the value of the information available to them.

Gerber, Mans-Kemp, and Schlechter (2013) contend that student engagement is vital for student success. Further, they suggest that "student engagement can be used as a proxy to describe how well or thoroughly students participate in daily academic life, which includes academic activities such as the completion of homework assignments, studying for tests and attending classes" (p. 259). So the question remains: what are the best practices we can employ to offer a supportive environment that facilitates student engagement? This is not only a question for those who teach, but also for those who learn. Coral Cara (2013) writes "both educators and students need to take responsibility in a supportive learning community since all have the right and also the responsibility to ensure maximal conditions for teaching and learning" (p. 24).

In this chapter, the authors consider differing approaches to student engagement; including discussion and writing opportunities, as well as creative access into course concepts through technologically based response methods that encourage classroom discussion. Chantel White suggests integrating real-time polling into classroom discussions. Students engage by participating in a "free text poll" that collects and synthesizes their responses, so that instructors may address student comments from the word cloud, thus allowing students to speak in more than one venue. Helene Arbouet Harte introduces us to an electronic "active student response system" that helps even the most reluctant discussant share his or her views with the class. Efua Akoma offers examples of classroom exercises and games that add an interactive component to teaching and learning. Further, Akoma teams up with Nichole-Boutee-Heiniluoma to offer valuable insight into student-based responsibilities for attaining success in writing by avoiding unnecessary paths of plagiarism or using non-academic sources, and instead, taking advantage of writing resources they may not know they have. Further, they share quick tips that students can use to enhance their time management skills.

Angela Miller describes an interactive process in which students sort words to identify patterns that exist in the content. This innovative activity can provide students "opportunities to engage with their peers in order to think more deeply about the terms and concepts." Rhonda Wrzenski shares insight into helping students comprehend scholarly research by offering them an organizational tool for consistency and clarity. Additionally, she describes the impact of a quick tip for addressing test anxiety and increasing exam preparation that has found true success in her classroom. In a discussion of knowledge surveys, Amy E. Bentz presents a practical approach for students to assess their understanding of course content, so they may target those areas in which they need more clarification.

Whatever the method, creating a supportive environment of trust and empowerment that enhances student success is vital. This chapter offers valuable contributions into an evolving discussion and significant pedagogical need.

References

Cara, C. (2013). Empowering many: Creating student engagement in changing Imes. *Global Studies Journal*, 5(4), 21–36.

Gerber, C., Mans-Kemp, N., & Schlechter, A. (2013). Investigating the moderating effect of student engagement on academic performance. *Acta Academica*, 45(4), 256–274.

LORI MONTALBANO
GOVERNORS STATE UNIVERSITY

ALL TOGETHER NOW! ENGAGING COLLEGE STUDENTS WITH ACTIVE STUDENT RESPONSE

HELENE ARBOUET HARTE
UNIVERSITY OF CINCINNATI BLUE ASH COLLEGE

Dr. Harte taught as an adjunct faculty member for 6 years. She is currently a program coordinator, assisting with hiring, orienting, and providing peer reviews for adjunct faculty.

Keywords: Engagement, Active Student Response, Clickers

Framework

Class begins and the instructor uses a relevant quote or comic strip for an interest catch. She invites the class to respond as to how the quote might be connected to the readings and topic for the day. Mia sits in the front row and her hand goes shooting up. She shares her insight. Throughout class whenever open-ended questions are posed, there is either silence or a response from a single student, often the same student.

In spite of using humor, providing adequate wait time, and making connections to the real world, many students do not respond during lecture. The instructor does not lecture for the whole class session and sees students participate in small groups. She would like the lecture to be more interactive in order to check for understanding and keep students on task.

Making it Work

Having some form of active student response during lecture may help with addressing student issues in terms of the need for timely feedback. Active student response requires students to respond in an observable way during instruction (Heward, 2013). It is an easy way to engage students. According to Bain (2012) effective college instructors obtain and maintain the attention of students, provide ways for students to commit to the class, and get students to engage in discussion. Active student response provides opportunities for all of these things. Classroom response systems may be electronic and record student responses to questions which can then be displayed to the class. One benefit is that the responses can be anonymous for sensitive or potentially embarrassing class issues, but everyone can still participate.

In a course on human sexuality that used a classroom response system, students indicated an increased comfort level with participating, increased likelihood of responding honestly, and helpfulness in staying engaged with the course material (Vail-Smith, Blumell, & Elmore, 2006). In an examination of another form of active student response (response cards), students reported not only increased responding, but also improved retention and learning during instruction (Musti-Rao, Kroeger, & Schumacher-Dyke, 2008). Response cards are not only preferred to raising hands and waiting to be selected, but also associated with higher scores on quizzes and tests (Heward, 1997). An additional benefit may be classroom management. Because students are engaged, writing, typing or clicking their responses, there may be fewer issues with off-task behavior such as texting. Incorporating ways to have the entire class respond involves a simple process.

Build in opportunities to respond during lecture. Ask a question or provide a prompt related to the content.

· · · · · · · · · · ·

Build in opportunities to respond during lecture. Ask a question or provide a prompt related to the content. Use a tool that allows all students to respond at once. Check the responses and tie them back to the lecture content. Correct any errors or misconceptions. Engage in a whole group discussion about the individual responses. This process should allow you to briefly assess students' understanding as well as provide them with feedback. Select the form of response that works best for you. It can be no tech, low tech, or high tech. Below are some examples of options for active student response.

- Pre-printed cards can be used. These may include one response on one side and the opposing response on the other (Ex: Yes/No or True/False).
- Index cards and markers allow students to write their responses and hold them up for the instructor to see.
- With dry-erase boards and dry-erase markers student write their responses and hold them up for the instructor to see.

- Tools such as Clickers http://www1.iclicker.com/ may be available through your college. With this tool students select a response to a question posed. An online alternative is Poll Everywhere: http://www.pollevery where.com/.
- Using a free online tool such as Today's Meet, https://todaysmeet.com/, or Lino, http://en.linoit.com/, allows students to type responses using a laptop or cell phone.

In my courses I use 9x12 dry-erase boards because they do not require any special materials, training, or access to technology. They do not require students to pay additional fees. In addition there is not a great need for storage, when office space may be limited or unavailable. A canvas bag or rolling crate is sufficient for storing and transporting materials

My experience has been consistent with the research literature. Students comment on class sessions where we do not use dry-erase boards or some form of active student response. They ask when we will use them again. In student evaluations and conversations before and after class, students comment that it is helpful to be "forced" to participate.

Future Implications

Once the technique of active student response is successfully incorporated into lecture, it could be extended by varying the response methods. It could also be turned into a partner or small group activity to encourage students to engage with one another. Initial responses allow for identification, recall and summary, but conversing with peers may allow for debate, deeper analysis, and synthesis of ideas. Providing opportunities for students to be actively engaged and respond can make lecture more of a dialogue rather than simply a monologue.

References

Bain, K. (2012). *What the best college students do*. Cambridge, Massachusetts: The Belknap Press of Harvard University Press.

Heward, W. L. (1997). Four validated instructional strategies. *Behavior and Social Issues, 7*(1), 43–51.

Heward, W.L. (2013). Exceptional children: *An introduction to special education* (10th Ed.). Upper Saddle River, NJ: Pearson Education, Inc.

Musti-Rao, S., Kroeger, S. D., & Schumacher-Dyke, K. (2008). Using guided notes and response cards at the postsecondary level. *Teacher Education & Special Education, 31*(3), 149–163.

Vail-Smith, K., Blumell, C., & Elmore, B. (2006). Using a "classroom response system" to improve active student participation in a large sexual health class. *American Journal of Sexuality Education, 1*(2), 47–54. doi:10.1300/J455v01n04_04

ATTENDANCE: WHEN "BUILD IT AND THEY WILL COME" DOESN'T WORK

KIMBERLY T. OLIVARES
INDIANA UNIVERSITY

Kimberly holds a MA in Student Affairs and Higher Education. She joined IU as an academic advisor and waded into the forum of teaching freshman seminars and Organizational Behavior as an adjunct. She currently works to support the teaching mission of IU on all eight of its campuses with FACET.

Keywords: Attendance, Strategies, Engagement

Framework

Every faculty member faces the attendance issue at some point. Before entering the classroom to teach for the first time, you might actually pray that no students show up. But before too long, you realize they need to be there, in the seat (or at the computer), engaging with the material. So how do you get them to come to class? There are many answers and you must find what works for you and what you are comfortable with as an instructor.

Making It Work

Here are a few ideas that I have tried in my classes:
1. ATTENDANCE IS MANDATORY! Think carefully before you put this statement in your syllabus. These

are adults in your classroom; can you force someone to attend? If you have forced them, will they be motivated to learn while there or just taking up space? What if they do miss class—do you want to hear the reason? Although, some of the reasons can be quite entertaining.

2. Grade class participation. Obviously you need to be physically present to participate in class. This sounds great but then you are in the situation of gauging what is "participation"—is it enough just to be present or do they have to respond to a particular number of questions—who is counting this and tabulating it. That would be YOU! There is definitely room to improve this idea.

3. Test on material that was mentioned in class and not in the book. This is brilliant as long as you have control over your tests and assignments but you might be teaching a course with multiple sections and the book, tests, etc., have been handed to you with no opportunity for you to alter them for your section of the course.

4. Using in-class quizzes to take attendance, assess learning and motivate students to attend. This is a good option but initially more work for you in setting up and grading quizzes. If the quiz is a good assessment of student learning and you can use it for both purposes then this might be your solution but if it is only for forcing attendance then it might not be worthwhile.

5. Develop a scale for absences. In my courses, students were permitted to miss 2 class sessions before they were penalized with the loss of a letter grade. I informed them that I didn't care what the reason of the absence was; if they knew they needed to travel and miss class—plan accordingly.

Future Implications

There is no right answer. This issue will continue to plague instructors for all of history, but you need to test the waters and find an option that works for you and your method of teaching.

MAKING COURSE CONTENT MORE ENGAGING!

EFUA AKOMA
ASHFORD UNIVERSITY

Dr. Efua Akoma has been teaching as both an adjunct and full-time instructor in sociology departments for the past 10 years.

Keywords: Engagement, PowerPoint, Games

One element that is essential to student success in the classroom is full engagement with the required material presented in the course. But do you feel like your students are not reading the required material? Worse yet, are their submissions demonstrating they are not reading or utilizing the required material? There are ways to enhance their engagement with the course content. If you are in an online learning environment, send them on a treasure hunt for elements of the course you know will be critical to their success throughout the class. If you are teaching in the traditional classroom, you can also send them on a treasure hunt in the syllabus and the course text.

Another great tool is to create crossword puzzles for your content that you can use in future courses. There are a number of easy and free programs that will assist you in creating the crossword puzzles, so it is not as difficult as you may think.

PowerPoint presentations have become a staple in many courses. Yes, there are some excellent presentations out there, and instructors have become creative with the many options for PowerPoints. However, there are some other options that can jazz up the presentation of your content and can hold your student's attention in a major way. Powtoon. com has become a favorite of late. It is still in the beta stage, so some elements may change as they receive feedback, but it is already a wonderful tool for presenting information. This tool presents information in an animated form, from cartoons to something similar to those handwritten presentations seen all over the Internet. Powtoon has a number of templates to choose from or you can create your own. The free version allows the creation of a 5-minute presentation; ample time to create something interesting and meaningful for your students. Use the voice-over option as a way to further establish a relationship with your students in an online learning environment. Remember to upload music and images to accompany course content in the presentation.

Powtoon is beneficial for introducing information to students by tapping into a variety of learning styles.

Reference

www.powtoon.com

DEEPENING CONCEPTUAL KNOWLEDGE AND CONTENT VOCABULARY THROUGH WORD SORTING

ANGELA MILLER
UNIVERSITY OF CINCINNATI

Dr. Miller taught education courses as an adjunct at three different universities for seven years. As a full-time faculty member and chair, she supervised and mentored adjuncts in the undergraduate education department.

Keywords: Content Development, Formative Assessment

Having taught many courses at both the undergraduate and graduate level as an adjunct, I have found that while many students come to class fully prepared and take the initiative to immerse themselves in the course, there are still, unfortunately, just as many students who are unwilling (or unable) to read the text, participate in discussions in the classroom, and ask questions to clarify their understanding. While quizzes and tests may eventually uncover the students' lack of subject knowledge, their limited familiarity with academic or content vocabulary, or their inability to make meaningful connections, these summative assessments do not increase the probability of content mastery by the end of the term. In fact, by the time summative assessments are completed and graded, the course has moved on, and before long, many students find themselves swimming in a sea of confusion, discouragement, and potential failure. Finding formative assessments that are interesting to adult students and encouraging them to engage with the course material and one another is not easy. One activity I discovered that has worked extremely well is word sorting (Bear, Invernizzi, Templeton, & Johnston, 2012). Originally developed as a developmental word study activity in order to promote word consciousness at the letter and sound level with young children, I have adapted the method to include academic vocabulary, content terminology, and pertinent names and phrases from the course.

The process of sorting words into various categories is relatively simple. Students receive a stack of cards that contain the words, terms, names, or content phrases. Students must then figure out the patterns that exist within the stack of cards and sort them accordingly. While categorizing these cards by certain elements, students begin to make connections, construct their own knowledge, talk about unfamiliar terms, and refer back to their textbook if necessary. This method of learning contrasts significantly to the rote review or test preparation activities that normally precede the implementation of summative assessments. It allows for the instructor to move about the room in order to provide feedback and clarification, and it provides students with opportunities to ask questions and think about content in new ways. Additionally, the instructor may challenge the organizational structure or ask the students to explain the reasoning behind the classifications. In this way, the instructor will glean information that may lead to occasions for resolving student misconceptions.

Students can be required to do a closed sort or an open sort. A closed sort is one in which the instructor provides the category headings under which the other words will be sorted; because the conceptual structure is predetermined, it is easier for students to complete. An instructor may choose to start with closed sorts before moving on to open sorts. An open sort is one in which no headings are provided. The students, after sorting the words according to their understanding, will need to provide the category titles. As the instructor moves around the room, she may choose to ask questions regarding why words have been grouped together or to require students to explain their understanding. Often, during the secondary process of explicating the chosen organization, students will recognize their own errors or make changes as they talk through the categories.

One example I can provide is when teaching a literacy theory course, the textbook chosen by the college (Tracey & Morrow, 2012) begins by providing the four foundational philosophies and placing them in historical context. The first word sort I developed for the students to complete was a closed sort where the category headings were the four foundational philosophies: Mental Discipline Theory, Associationism, Unfoldment Theory, and Structuralism. The cards to be sorted included the names of philosophers, theorists, and researchers associated with those philosophies (e.g., Aristotle, John Locke, Jean-Jacques Rousseau, James Cattell); descriptive phrases of the basic tenets of each philosophies such as "mind is a muscle," "events categorized in the mind," "cultivation of interest and passion," and "perception-oriented;" instructional techniques related to the philosophies (e.g., "rote memorization," "brainstorming activities," "graphic organizers," "literacy learning centers," "using pointers for early readers"); and finally cards that indicate approximate date ranges for the popularity of the philosophies.

Students with whom I have used word sorting report that it has helped them work with the material in more meaningful ways. Most have indicated on course evaluations that word sorting provides them with opportunities to engage with their peers in order to think more deeply about the terms and concepts. It has been my experience that classes that have been provided opportunities to word sort prior to testing usually perform better on assessments and writing assignments. Additionally, many of my students (all of whom are current or future educators) suggest that the instructional strategy is one that they hope to utilize in their own classrooms.

While I have used the word sorting strategy in almost all of my classes, I have found that the best word sorts are those that require students to work with more than simple terms. While mastering content vocabulary is critical to student success, word sorts that do little more than match terms to definitions do not provide students with enough depth and breadth of conceptual information to make meaningful and lasting connections. Conceptual word sorting can be used as advanced organizers for anticipating new course reading, they can be revisited and refined after reading or lecture, and they can be used as a formative assessment prior to testing.

References

Bear, D. R., Invernizzi, M., Templeton, S., & Johnston, F. (2012). *Words their way: Word study for phonics, vocabulary, and spelling instruction*. Boston: Pearson, Inc.

Tracey, D., & Morrow, L.M. (2012). *Lenses on reading: An introduction to theories and models*. New York: The Guilford Press.

HELPING STUDENTS COMPREHEND SCHOLARLY RESEARCH

RHONDA WRZENSKI
INDIANA UNIVERSITY SOUTHEAST

Dr. Wrzenski has been an assistant faculty member in political science at Indiana University Southeast since 2010. Prior to this, she served as an adjunct faculty member at Baker University. As an adjunct, she taught sections in both political science and critical thinking and effective writing.

Keywords: Learning Research Structure, Reading Comprehension

Framework

When I started teaching undergraduates, I incorporated scholarly journal articles into their typical reading load. I wanted students to gain some exposure to research and to theories in our discipline. I also hoped that reading these pieces would facilitate a greater understanding of research structure they could apply in their capstone course and/ or in graduate school. Finally, I wanted students to learn to think critically by critiquing these pieces and generating new research ideas. Students found this reading very difficult and tedious but I still felt the acquisition of these skills and concepts outweighed the frustration. My goal is to help students better comprehend the material by getting them to compartmentalize the articles into manageable chunks. This also ensured a higher quality of discussion as submitting these summaries counted as an assignment and students could not complete the summary without having done a careful reading of the material.

Making it Work

To foster better reading comprehension, I created and shared an electronic template that students used to summarize or "autopsy" each journal article. At the top of the Word document template, students type out the full journal article citation. Then, they enter information into the corresponding spaces under the headings for: the main research question(s), the hypotheses and theoretical context, the data and methods, the findings, and the conclusion. Finally, they have space to comment on the article, to critique the article, and to provide future research ideas. Students are instructed that a thorough summary is typically one to two single-spaced typed pages.

Future Implications

After my first semester requiring these summaries, I made adjustments in implementation for subsequent semesters. First, I made becoming more adept at reading and understanding the content and structure of scholarly literature one of my course goals. I also spent part of class time explaining how I felt this exercise would benefit the students and why it was one of my goals. When students felt discouraged I reassured them that this was a challenging task and one that takes practice to master. As most students saw their grades improve over the semester, they gained more confidence and some enjoyed the way the exercise turned the reading

material into one big scavenger hunt. Besides making this a course goal, prior to their first journal reading, I posted a completed summary of the article along with the template. This allowed students to reference the documents as they were reading the piece and to go back to them throughout the semester. Finally, I reserved class time for students to work in small groups on the next reading. I touched base with each group as they completed the template and we finished the class by going through the template as a group. From here, depending on class size and the number of articles assigned, students were usually broken into groups and assigned specific articles over the semester to be completed individually, but discussed collectively.

Example of Article Summary Template
ARTICLE CITATION– Author, A. A., Author, B. B., & Author, C. C. (Year). Title of article. Title of Periodical, volume number(issue number), pages. http://dx.doi.org/xx.xxx/yyyyy

---

DESCRIPTION/SUMMARY
1. Main Research Question(s)
    -
    -
2. Hypotheses and Theoretical Context
3. Data and Methods
4. Findings
5. Conclusions
6. Comments/Critiques/Future Research Ideas

Knowledge Surveys: A Self-Assessment Tool

Amy E. Bentz
Western Michigan University

Dr. Bentz is a former high school science teacher and has previously served as an adjunct faculty member for two years. Dr. Bentz is currently a faculty specialist in Teaching, Learning, and Educational Studies at Western Michigan University.

Keywords: Formative Assessment, Knowledge Survey, Self-Assessment

Framework

In my experience, it is not uncommon for students to ask for a "study guide" to help them prepare for upcoming tests. Instead of simply providing students with a study guide at the

end of the unit, I wanted to give students a tool they could use throughout the unit to help them self-assess their understanding. I started to look for additional tools that would not only encourage the process of self-assessment, but do so by explicitly promoting the communication of clear learning objectives. I came across a tool called a knowledge survey (Nuhfer, 1993).

Making it Work

Nuhfer (1996) describes a knowledge survey as a list of questions, which vary in cognitive complexity, and focus on the important concepts covered in the course. The knowledge survey is typically given at the beginning of the learning cycle, revisited when applicable throughout the learning cycle, and then again at the end of the learning cycle. Rather than answering the questions on the knowledge survey, students are asked to rate their current understanding using the following scale: (1) I'm confused! I don't understand this topic. (2) I have a good understanding of the topic, but I still have some questions. (3) I can answer this question

correctly on a test. Using this tool can encourage students to seek additional support on the areas they feel they need extra help. Here is an example of a few knowledge survey questions.

Future Implications

Feedback from my students regarding the use of knowledge surveys has been overall positive. The students appreciate the structured guidance and are encouraged by the opportunity to self-assess their understanding. In the future, I believe it would be helpful to add an additional option to the ranking scale: (4) I can teach this to a fellow peer. For many, teaching a concept to another person is an added step to fully understanding a concept. Perhaps this type of self-assessment would also be beneficial for our students.

Knowledge Survey Questions:	(1) I don't understand	(2) I somewhat understand	(3) I fully understand
How has sea level changed over the past 25,000 years?			
Explain why tectonics is thought to be a driving force of long-term sea level change.			
Describe the effects of global change on the coastlines of the eastern United States.			
Describe how the magnitude and timing of sea level changes help provide insight into Earth's climate history.			

Figure 2.1. A self-assessment tool

References

Nuhfer, E. B. (1996). The place of formative evaluations in assessment and ways to reap their benefits. *Journal of Geoscience Education, 44*(4), 385–394.

Nuhfer, E. (1993). Bottom-line disclosure and assessment. *Teaching Professor, 7*(7), 8.

QUICK TIPS FOR TIME MANAGEMENT

EFUA AKOMA
ASHFORD UNIVERSITY

Dr. Efua Akoma has been teaching as both an adjunct and full-time instructor in sociology departments for the past 10 years.

NICHOLE BOUTTE-HEINILUOMA
ASHFORD UNIVERSITY

Dr. Boutte-Heiniluoma has been teaching both political science and sociology for the past 6 years.

Keywords: Time Management, Productivity

With the many responsibilities of today's student, time management can be a real challenge. This is especially true for those who are working, have families, and/or have assumed other responsibilities that may conflict with school. In short, time is a fixed entity. We all have the same amount in each day, yet some are able to do so much while others accomplish less. One difference between these two types of people may lie in their ability (or inability) to manage choices with respect to the time allocated for individual task completion. Providing students with strategies for time management can help reduce stress, thereby enabling goal attainment across a number of activities. This guide lists 10 tips that we share with students in our respective classrooms.

Avoid procrastination. Procrastination can create a snowball effect, so don't be the "Pro" in procrastination. Once you have access to the schedule and syllabus, plug the due dates for your required work into a calendar, giving yourself time to complete, review, and edit before assignment submission. Once you have set your assignment schedule, plug in study, work, play and even family times accordingly. From there, stick to the plan. Good planning yields good results.

Create a to-do list. While this may seem like one more thing to do, it will help you organize your tasks and make sure you are not forgetting anything. Once you have your schedule, create a to-do list that includes all of the individual tasks you will need to accomplish in order to be efficient and effective. For example, for each assignment, include trips to the library, research and writing time, group work, etc., necessary for completion. Make sure you prioritize your activities from most important to the least, keeping in mind your ultimate goals.

Review your list at the end of each day, praising yourself for those things accomplished and reassessing those things you did not attain. If necessary, place them at the beginning of the next day's list.

Find the time of day you are the most productive. Being at your best can improve your productivity substantially. Set some of this time aside to work on school related actvities. Any dedicated time is better than scrounging up time where you can.

Create a work space. You can train your brain to jump-start if you dedicate a specific area in which you will engage in work. Consistently work in that dedicated space; doing so can help you get into the work groove more quickly.

Get a good night's sleep. It might seem silly, but make sure to schedule your sleep too. Know what your limits are in the event you need to minimize this element of your life. If sleep is calling and you haven't gotten everything done, your to-do list may spill over to the next day and that is okay. Reprioritize the list for the next day and keep moving forward.

Getting sidetracked. If you feel you are not on task, revisit your to-do list. Mark off the items completed and move on to the next item on the list. Getting sidetracked is easier than ever with technology, family, work, play, each of which adds to the ease of getting sidetracked. When conducting research online, avoid social networking sites and webpages that are not focused on you or your success.

Saying yes could stall your progress. Your time is precious so you must find ways to get the most out of what you have, especially as you pursue a degree that positively impacts the path you are trying to be on. Having to say no is especially difficult when friends and family ask, but it is

We all
have the
same amount
in each day.

okay, and often necessary. In those times where compromise is needed, when 'no' is simply not an acceptable response, offer "let's schedule something" and work it into your calendar.

Travel with your work. Many people have smart phones and can download the schools' app if they are taking online courses, which can allow you to engage in your discussion questions or retrieve written assignment instructions so you can begin thinking about your paper topic and approaches to writing it. Many students benefit from utilizing online apps or other resources where they can create, retrieve and edit assignments across various devices. In addition, e-mailing yourself assignments each time you revise can save hours of time and frustration if other forms of technology are lost, stolen or corrupted.

Be a good student. Going to class, being on time, participating in class, and staying on top of your work lend themselves to you being viewed favorably by your instructor. Thus, should emergencies arise, he/she might be willing to work with you. Instructors cannot assist if they do not know what is going on. Make sure you have located your instructor's contact information and have it handy should you need it. Do not wait until there is a problem to seek guidance, but if one arises, make sure you make your instructor aware.

Proper planning. See all of the above.

Managing one's time is not as easy as it seems. However, once this process is started, it becomes easier to navigate the hurdles that life throws in our way. Once incorporated these tips are useful for students in every discipline and learning environment.

ENCOURAGING CLASSROOM DISCUSSION WITH REAL-TIME POLLING

CHANTEL E. WHITE
INDIANA UNIVERSITY SOUTH BEND

Dr. White has taught introductory courses in cultural anthropology, archaeology, and physical anthropology in the Department of Sociology and Anthropology at IUSB for the past two years.

Keywords: Real-Time Polling, Classroom Participation, Text Messaging

Framework

Introductory courses in anthropology and other social sciences provide students with a greater understanding of the human experience through an examination of cultures across the world. An important step in developing an awareness and appreciation for human diversity occurs when students begin to reconsider their own assumptions through classroom discussion. It can be difficult to initiate participation in these discussions when students' long-held beliefs are questioned or viewed in a new light. One particularly useful means of increasing student participation in these debates is to initiate classroom discussions with real-time polling, a technique that offers anonymity to students and provides immediate, real-time feedback for instructors.

Making It Work

The principle of real-time polling is quite simple. Through an online website such as Poll Everywhere (http://poll everywhere.com) instructors can present a question to the class and allow students to respond via anonymous text message. After a question is asked, students take a moment to reflect and then choose from a series of multiple-choice options provided by the instructor. They can then access their cell phones and send a text message to a secure number generated by the polling website. As students text in their multiple-choice responses, the polling website will generate a bar graph in real time indicating the percentage of students who have chosen each option. These graphics are easily embedded in presentations or displayed directly through the polling website during lecture.

An instructor can also reframe the question as a "free text poll" to encourage open-ended responses from students. For example, a general question about a discussion topic such as "What is your opinion on US immigration laws?" allows students to submit individually written text responses. As each text is received by the polling website, a unique word cloud displaying students' text messages will be generated in real time. The word cloud is a useful visual tool for students to view other students' opinions on the subject. Word clouds can help an instructor determine whether more time should be spent reviewing the readings and background information. They also display important patterns in student responses which can be acknowledged and examined.

Students may not always feel comfortable speaking up.

• • • • • • • • • • • •

Identifying patterns in student responses is key to beginning a meaningful classroom discussion. For example, regarding the polling question on immigration, I compare students' real-time responses to state and national polls on immigration policies. I find these types of comparisons between classroom opinions and larger polls help generate discussion as students seek to explain why differences exist and to understand viewpoints distinct from their own.

Students may not always feel comfortable speaking up about their personal beliefs. They are much more willing to comment on why trends in classroom opinions might exist and how experiences in their community have shaped public opinion. More importantly, I find that students begin to consider the reasoning behind their own opinions and reflect on "how they know what they know"—that is, their own social, political, and religious affiliations, which influence long-held beliefs on important topics.

Future Implications

I find real-time polls to be particularly useful as a means of breaking up lecture time and changing pace to engage all students in an activity. Moreover, students are allowed to briefly use their phones in the classroom, which lends a bit of novelty to the activity, as does the appearance of students' text messages appearing on the classroom screen. One difficulty I encountered with online polling concerns open-ended questions. Students sometimes feel as though they have already "contributed" via their text message and need not take part in the subsequent discussion. This situation can be easily remedied by asking students to identify specific patterns or similarities in their word cloud responses, and by following up with more pointed questions about what these patterns might tell us about the group as a whole. In the future, I plan to use real-time polls to gauge student preparation for exams and to receive informal mid-semester feedback from students on my courses.

STUDENT AFFAIRS 101

KIMBERLY T. OLIVARES
INDIANA UNIVERSITY

Kimberly holds a MA in Student Affairs and Higher Education. She joined IU as an academic advisor and waded into the forum of teaching freshman seminars and Organizational Behavior as an adjunct. She currently works to support the teaching mission of IU on all eight of its campuses with FACET.

Keywords: Student Affairs, Student Aid, Financial Aid, Adaptive Services, Disability, Career Services, Academic Advising

Framework

So as a good teacher you have bonded with some of your students despite arriving at class from your day job with only minutes to spare. These students are sharing their lives with you, their aspirations, their challenges … you may feel ill-equipped to respond to all of these issues. There are people on campus to help you; you just need to know where to look.

Making it Work

Student Affairs is an often misunderstood or unknown entity for adjuncts and lecturers who don't spend their time on campus regularly and depending on how your were hired to teach, you may or may not have been given an orientation to the campus and teaching. If you were oriented that isn't a guarantee you were told about the myriad of offices and support services across campus that help students successfully navigate their college experience. These offices—Career Services, Psychological Services, Adaptive Education, Academic Advising, Financial Aid, to name a few—are what encompass the student affairs profession. I will share a few situations you might encounter in class and the offices on your campus you might refer the student to or ask for help yourself in how to best advise a student.

So you have a student that is very active in classroom participation, adds to the conversation on nearly every topic in class with meaningful insights and questions but his or her test or quiz scores don't reflect what they know (and what you know they know). There could be any number of things going on with this student and obviously you want to inquire with them first. You may find that they have a diagnosed learning disability but have not mentioned this to anyone on campus. This is a time to refer the student to the office of Adaptive Education on your campus. It might appear under different names: Adaptive Services, Disability Resource Center, or Educational Services. If you can't locate it, I would bet a call to any academic advisor on your campus would yield the correct office and contact person. The office of Adaptive Education typically is able to help a student with documented disabilities (physical, mental, emotional) to access the correct accommodations and services on campus to ensure their success. This might be a temporary issue of a student dealing with a health crisis in the short term that needs assistances getting to and from class; a student with a learning disability that needs extra time with testing or to have tests read to them; or a student with visual impairments might arrange to take exams on computers in the Adaptive Services offices that are modified with programs that allow them to enlarge the text.

Mental health is quickly becoming a large concern on campuses across the country. Unfortunately, we read headlines all too frequently about students that have committed suicide or have become violent on campus. Many universities and colleges have a unit to provide psychological services to students and staff. These units will typically be able to assess if there is an immediate threat and provide appropriate interventions or continued counseling. This particular office might also be called on to help diagnose students with various learning disabilities and can provide testing to assess their disabilities.

One of the more important services that students all too frequently don't use is an academic advisor. These professionals can not only help a student navigate course selection and sequencing but aid in getting transfer courses to count toward a degree requirement, refer a student to another service on campus or in the community, and encourage students to take a holistic approach to their college career that includes not only academics but internships, sports, and student interest groups.

Just as adjuncts sometimes struggle to make ends meet, we are finding with more frequency that students are also struggling financially. It might be worth a trip to the financial aid office for a student to investigate if they qualify for more grant money, loan money (if the situation is dire), or work-study opportunities. On some campuses, students have opened up food pantries to help students and staff get through the leaner times without being hungry.

Future Implications

Obviously, there is no way to prepare you for every eventuality that might come up with students as you build a learning community with them but there are normally resources on each campus to offer support. I encourage you to find a good academic advisor in the unit you teach for and use this person as a resource to help you help your students.

One of the more important services that students all too frequently don't use is an academic advisor. These professionals can not only help a student navigate course selection...

STUDENT WRITING CHALLENGES

EFUA AKOMA
ASHFORD UNIVERSITY

Dr. Efua Akoma has been teaching as both an adjunct and full-time instructor in sociology departments for the past 10 years.

NICHOLE BOUTTE-HEINILUOMA
ASHFORD UNIVERSITY

Dr. Boutte-Heiniluoma has been teaching both political science and sociology for the past 6 years.

Keywords: Plagiarism, Academic Resources, Writing Resources

Many students, often unsure of their writing skills, resort to using shortcuts to complete assignments. These shortcuts are then noted by faculty as plagiarism, using non-scholarly resources, and or failing to refer to appropriate resources to aid in the writing process. This guide is intended to be a resource for faculty faced with any of these challenges during the grading process.

Plagiarism

Plagiarism is a process in which students engage either knowingly or unintentionally. The former is considered cheating; the latter can be used as a teaching moment. In all cases, the first line of defense is to clearly define plagiarism on each class syllabus. Instructors should provide information about where to find additional resources, such as plagiarism.org, APAStyle.org or Purdue Owl. Syllabi should suggest that students utilize a plagiarism detection program prior to submitting their work. A final pre-assignment approach is to provide a short writing exercise that allows students to practice their paraphrasing skills using a selected piece of writing in order to receive instructor feedback on their effort.

Though faculty may be proactive in their approaches to educating students about plagiarism, there remains the need to accurately and consistently identify when the efforts of others are not properly cited. There are detection programs, such as Turnitin.com, that check papers against a large database using quality assurance systems. Regardless of the program used it remains the responsibility of the faculty member to verify citations are present. In addition, some programs may only be available through purchase. Plagtracker.com is free and available to students and instructors and, when used properly, can help save time, effort and frustration for both. In all instances, faculty should refer to the policy of their respective university.

Scholarly and non-academic/popular resources

Faculty often find popular media and other non-academic resources used to substantiate an argument. Opinions and generalizations are numerous and, because they are often reinforced in several kinds of media, students unquestioningly assume their truth and use them to support assertions in academic assignments. To help students avoid this pitfall, faculty can include links to reliable academic and other acceptable resources in course syllabi. In addition, faculty can include charts that highlight the differences between various kinds of publications and media resources. Charts should also include information about the purpose of the publications, the intended audiences, reliability and validity of sources cited, the manuscript review process, and the credibility of the publishing company or organization.

Because the internet has become such a vast source of information, students will often turn to search engines to find information to substantiate their arguments. In addition to the information mentioned above, helping students understand the domain name in the address of an Internet site can help you determine the purpose of the site and how that relates to the information provided there. Distinguishing between a .com, .org, .edu, .gov, .mil, and .net could make a huge difference in how they can utilize the information.

Writing resources

There are a number of appropriate resources to which students have access. The key is letting them know they exist. For example, instructing students about conducting an internet search for writing style information should include suggestions about narrowing the parameters through the use of specifics, i.e., APA or MLA, versus encompassing terms such as "writing styles." In addition, university writing centers, tutors, or library assistants can assist students with editing, the revision process, and finding resources to improve their writing skills.

Because students have different ways of learning, it is important to provide powerful visual supports in addition to lecturing. In other words, "seeing is believing." Faculty can provide sample papers with correct formatting as a way to illustrate proper formatting and paper construction. Examples should include introductions, strong relevant thesis, transitional sentences, quoting, citing, well-crafted conclusion, and relevant scholarly references.

Students come to learn but they have varying levels of knowledge as it relates to writing. We know every student is different and our objective should be to meet them where they are and bring them to a new level of understanding and performance. These quick tips can assist them in their journey to becoming a better writer!

||||||||||||||||||||||||||||||||||||||||||||||||||||||||||||||||||||||||||||||||||||||||||||||||||||||||||||||||||||||||||||||||||||||||||||||||||||||||||||||||||||||||||||||

ONE QUICK TIP FOR ADDRESSING TEST ANXIETY AND INCREASING EXAM PREPARATION

RHONDA WRZENSKI
INDIANA UNIVERSITY SOUTHEAST

Dr. Wrzenski has been an assistant faculty member in political science at Indiana University Southeast since 2010. Prior to this, she served as an adjunct faculty member at Baker University. As an adjunct, she taught sections in both political science and critical thinking and effective writing.

Keywords: Test Preparation, Test Anxiety, Study Aids

Framework

At the start of my teaching career, I was disappointed in student performance on exams. I felt that some students were not investing enough time into test preparation and were missing the connection between adequate preparation and success. I also had multiple conversations with students who expressed heavy test anxiety. These were students who often performed well on homework and regularly participated in class discussions but simply froze up on exams.

Making it Work

To address these problems, I began to allow students in my introductory classes to bring in one page of notes for the exam. Students were given clear guidelines for the notes page at the bottom of each exam review sheet. Essentially, the students were restricted to a standard 8.5 by 11 inch sheet of paper and were only allowed to write on one side of the page. The students were required to write their notes by hand onto the sheet of paper in either pen or pencil. The restriction on typed notes is connected to research that shows information retention is better when lecture notes are written by hand and subsequently reviewed (Mueller and Oppenheimer 2014; Carter and Van Matre, 1975). Finally, students were encouraged to fill the whole space but were cautioned to keep their handwriting legible and to keep the font size readable. In other words, students were urged to focus on the material they find especially difficult to remember. All notes pages were reviewed prior to the exam to ensure the rules were being followed. Students who needed to make adjustments in writing size were given this feedback on the first exam so they could modify their style for future notes pages. Each student submits their notes pages with their completed exams so the pages cannot be distributed to other students in future semesters.

After the first exam, I routinely get earnest appeals from students to continue the practice. In addition, I regularly see comments on my student evaluations of teaching that reinforce the practice. The average comment will state that the sheets helped with studying the material or eased test anxiety.

The benefits of allowing a notes page on exams: After implementing this strategy, I noticed that students began to see the connection between focused preparation and exam performance. They were given a tangible incentive to carefully examine the review sheet and to put time into studying for the exam. By keeping the aid to one page students knew they would have to make choices about what went on the page. If open notes were allowed, students might underprepare thinking they could simply look up whatever they needed to know. In effect, they might overestimate their ability to hunt down the information needed in a restricted timeframe. By keeping notes to one page, students have a more manageable aid and can feel less tense knowing they have a small security blanket with them. As a side benefit, students really concentrate their attention on the exam and on their notes and their eyes do not drift to other desks. In other words, I honestly feel the notes page can reduce the urge to cheat.

Future Implications

In the beginning of implementation, some students put in more time crafting their study aid than others. Although this is still true to some extent, I found I got better-quality notes pages when I provided examples of well-done notes pages for the whole class prior to the exams. This helps students better understand the font size I want them to use and gives them ideas about how to segment information by chapter using highlighters, boxes, etc. In essence, I learned that

students would often work harder and feel more confident in producing these sheets if they had good examples modeled for them.

This policy can also be used in upper-level sections. Students can be given anywhere from a half a page to a whole page of notes. To make this determination, you may want to consider the number of exams per semester, the amount of content covered on each exam, and the grade level of the average student in the course.

References

Carter, J., & Van Matre, N. (1975). Note taking versus note having. *Journal of Educational Psychology, 67*(6), 900–904. doi:10.1037/0022-0663.67.6.900

Mueller, P., & Oppenheimer, D. (2014). The pen is mightier than the keyboard: Advantages of longhand over laptop note taking. *Psychological Science, 25*(4). doi: 10.1177/0956797614524581. Retrieved from: http://pss.sagepub.com/content/early/2014/04/22/0956797614524581

In the beginning of implementation, some students put in more time crafting their study aid than others. Although this is still true to some extent, I found I got better-quality notes pages when I provided examples of well-done notes pages...

ADOPTING BEST PRACTICES

*E*ducators from a variety of disciplines often rely on storytelling as a foundation for successful teaching, using parables, historical events, myths, or personal history to instruct, illustrate, and guide (Zabel, 1991; Sanchez et al., 2009). For example, to illustrate the relationship between gender role socialization and the social structure, I tell stories about my own life. Jacobs (1998, p. 23) argues "By sharing ourselves, and opening up for critical reflection, we not only give students an additional text to read that facilitates understandings of course material, but we also help them practice pedagogy's project of deconstructing authority and resisting passive acceptance of knowledge/truth claims." Jacobs offers more sage advice from bell hooks:

> It is often productive if professors take the first risk, linking confessional narrative to academic discussions so as to show how experience can illuminate and enhance our understanding of academic material (1998, p. 223).

A review of the literature on teaching sociology reveals a litany of creative and innovative practices to assist novitiates, or what I have called elsewhere, "sociological virgins" (Gallmeier, 2005), in developing their sociological imaginations. These pedagogical techniques include: classroom debates (Hiller, 1974; Huyrn, 1986; Green & Klug, 1990; Crone, 1997), drama and theater (Parrott, 1987; Hardy, 1989), movies and documentaries (Smith, 1982; Prendergast, 1986; Burton, 1988; Valdez & Halley, 1999; Tipton & Tiemann, 1993), comic books (Hall & Lucal, 1999), photograph (Hanson, 2002), literature (Jones, 1974; Hendershott & Wright, 1993; Sullivan, 1982; Lena & London, 1979), music (Martinez, 1998; 1994; Ahlkvist, 1999), and even poetry (Miley, 1988; Moran, 1999).

Television is another excellent source of data to whet students' intellectual appetites and jump start critical thinking skills. Hess and Grant (1982) used prime time television programming to illustrate gender role behavior in American society. Others have followed their lead (Snow, 1982; Unnithan & Scheuble, 1982; Hood-Williams, 1986; Gallmeier, 2009), focusing on television news, soap operas, or television situation comedies to teach sociology of the family.

Drawing upon James Henslin's (1999) article "on Becoming Male," I share my life as a young boy. Students learn that at a relatively young age my brothers and I had the run of our neighborhood and the neighborhoods beyond our housing subdivision. I could go anywhere and was encouraged to do so. My sister's world, however, was limited to the front and back yards. When she complained, which she did often, she was simply told she was a girl and we were boys. I learned early on that I was one of the lucky ones, that the world was mine, and I shared it with other boys.

I move from the family and focus on the school as a socialization agent in our patriarchal society. I tell my students that from kindergarten through fourth grade my teachers were women and they called me "Chuckie." In fifth grade I got my first male teacher. I was no longer "Chuckie"—I was now "Mr. Gallmeier." I ask the class to raise their hands if their teacher was a woman in kindergarten and to keep them in the air as we walk through the various grades and to lower them only when they encountered their first male teacher. Students look around the room and observe a sea of hands stretched upward until they begin dropping around the fifth and sixth grade. We discuss how we learn subtly that when we are small we need a mother figure, a nurturer, and as we get older we need the authoritative figure of a man. By using what Jacobs (1998, p. 226) calls "the teacher as text," I am saying "This is how it is for me; use my experience as a guide to help figure out how it is for you" (Gallmeier, 2005, p. 89–90).

The examples provided above are just a few of the best practices sociologists use to introduce students to what Mills (1959) named the sociological imagination. He noted that using the sociological imagination demands a lot of practice and a lot of work. People do not naturally think like sociologists. Most people in our society believe that individuals choose their own destiny. Although it is true that individuals do make choices, they make them within the limits of the society in which they live. The ultimate goal is to use best practices that enable students to begin to understand the difference in using structural, rather than individual, explanations to explain social problems and complex social phenomena.

The best practices described in the essays and articles in this chapter of *Quick Hits* are excellent examples of pedagogical techniques to assist students in being successful in a variety of disciplines. Kille et al. discuss the use of the "The Five Rs" as an learning assessment tool and Janice Poston argues persuasively that forum postings should be used in online and hybrid courses to increase teaching presence which will ultimately contribute to student success. Professor O'Malley discusses the value of implementing seven principles to enhance active learning activities in traditional, hybrid, and online courses. Dr. Young's article introduces the use of Twitter as a best practice to "enhance classroom discussions during and after viewing a documentary film" and Professor Hasty describes the advantages of assigning students to a rich variety of field experiences in order to "provide real-life, concrete examples of course topics." Professor Guevara-Velez's Quick Hit lobbies for a model of a learning community in teacher preparation courses which emphasizes the importance of student/instructor mentorships. Professor Hajra recommends in her essay that students be allowed to grade their own exams to better understand the mistakes they are making, and finally, Professor Rogers argues for replacing conceptual learning in his macroeconomics classes with a full-class-participation experiment which more closely captures real world experiences.

Whether one is teaching sociology, merchandising, or macroeconomics, the goals are always the same. We need to create, employ, and share best practices so regardless of the discipline or subject matter our students will be successful. The Quick Hits in this chapter are all capable of accomplishing this important outcome.

References

Ahlkvist, J. (1999). Music and cultural analysis in the classroom: Introducing sociology through heavy metal. *Teaching Sociology, 27*, 26–144.

Burton, E. C. (1988). Sociology and the feature film. *Teaching Sociology, 16*, 263–271.

Crone, J.A. (1997). Using panel debates to increase student involvement in the introductory sociology class. *Teaching Sociology, 25*, 214–218

Gallmeier, C. P. (2009). From Father Knows Best to Will and Grace: Using television situation comedies to teach sociology of the family. *Journal for the Liberal Arts and Sciences, 13*(2), 24–39.

Gallmeier, C. P. (2005). Reflections on teaching: Introducing sociological virgins to the sociological imagination. *Sociological Focus, 38*(2), 83–93.

Green, C., & Hadley G. K. (1990). Hans O. Mauksch award presentation: Teaching critical thinking and writing through debates: An experimental evaluation. *Teaching Sociology, 18*, 462–471.

Hall, K. J., & Lucal, B. (1999). Tapping into parallel universes: Using superhero comic books in sociology courses. *Teaching Sociology, 27*, 60–66.

Hanson, C. M. (2002). A stop sign at the intersection of history and biography: Illustrating Mills imagination with depression-era photographs. *Teaching Sociology, 30,* 235–242.

Hardy, T. (1989). Toward a critical pedagogy in sociology in sociology through the use of drama. *Teaching Sociology, 17,* 226–231

Hendershott, A. & Wright, S. (1993). Bringing the sociological perspective into the interdisciplinary classroom through literature. *Teaching Sociology, 21,* 325–331.

Henslin, J. M. (1999. On becoming male: Reflections of a sociologist on childhood and early socialization. In James M. Henslin (Ed.), *Down to Earth Sociology.* New York: The Free Press.

Hess, D. J., & Grant, G.W. (1982). Prime-time television and gender-role behavior. *Teaching Sociology, 10,* 371–388.

Hiller, H. H. (1974). The sociological debate: Innovating with the pedagogical role. *Teaching Sociology, 2,* 123–132.

Hood-Williams, J. (1986). Soaps and the sociology of the family. *Teaching Sociology, 14,* 270–272.

Huryn, J. S. (1986). Debating as a teaching technique. *Teaching Sociology, 14,* 266–269.

Jacobs, W. R. (1986). The teacher as text: Using personal experiences to stimulate the sociological imagination. *Teaching Sociology, 26,* 222–228.

Jones, R. A. (1974). The use of literature in teaching introductory sociology: A case study. *Teaching Sociology, 2,* 176–177.

Lena, H.R., & London, B. (1978). An introduction to sociology through fiction: Using Kesey's One Flew over the Cuckoo's Nest. *Teaching Sociology, 6,* 123–132.

Martinez, T. A. (1988). Race and popular culture: Teaching African leadership styles through popular music. *Teaching Sociology, 26,* 207–214.

Miley, J. D. (1988). By its right name: The relevance for poetry for sociology. *Teaching Sociology, 16,* 173–176.

Mills, C. W. (1959). *The sociological imagination.* NY: Oxford University Press

Moran, T. P. (1999). Versifying your reading list: Using poetry to teach inequality. *Teaching Sociology, 27,* 110–125.

Parrott, A. (1987). Is Queen Victoria lecturing today? Teaching human sexuality using famous personalities. *Teaching Sociology, 15,* 257–262.

Prendergast, C. (1986). Cinema sociology: Cultivating the sociological imagination through popular film. *Teaching Sociology, 14,* 243–248.

Sanchez, T., Zam, G., & Lambert, J. (2009). Storytelling as an effective strategy in teaching character education in middle grades social studies. *Journal for the Liberal Arts and Sciences, 13*(2), 14–28.

Smith, D. D. (1982). Teaching undergraduate sociology through feature films. *Teaching Sociology, 10,* 98–101.

Snow, R. P. (1982). Teaching sociology though existing television programs. *Teaching Sociology, 10,* 353–360.

Sullivan, T. (1982). Introductory sociology through literature. *Teaching Sociology, 10,* 109–116.

Tipton, D. B., & Tiemann, K.A. (1993). Using the feature film to facilitate sociological thinking. *Teaching Sociology, 21,* 187–191.

Unnithan, N. P., & Scheuble, L. K. (1982). Evaluating an attempt at relevance: The use of news item analysis in introductory sociology. *Teaching Sociology, 10,* 399–405.

Zabel, M. (1991). Storytelling, myths, and folk tales: Strategies for multicultural inclusion. *Preventing School Failure, 36*(1), 32–34.

CHARLES P. GALLMEIER
INDIANA UNIVERSITY NORTHWEST

APPLYING THE FIVE RS TO TRADITIONAL ASSESSMENT

TARRYN KILLE
GRIFFITH AVIATION, GRIFFITH UNIVERSITY

Tarryn has been a tertiary educator for the past six years. As the director of Aviation Undergraduate Studies she supervised up to 10 adjunct lecturers each year.

PAUL BATES
GRIFFITH AVIATION, GRIFFITH UNIVERSITY

Paul is the head of Aviation at Griffith University. He has been teaching in tertiary programs for the past 30 years. Paul manages eight full-time lecturers and associate professors, including a pool of over 40 adjunct lecturers.

PATRICK S. MURRAY
GRIFFITH AVIATION, GRIFFITH UNIVERSITY

Patrick is the director of the Aerospace Strategic Study Centre at Griffith University. He has been a professional educator for over 30 years. While directing and teaching in postgraduate coursework and research programs, Patrick also supervises over 30 adjunct lecturers.

Keywords: Traditional Assessment, Deep Learning

Framework

When was the last time you found a student enthusiastically engaged in writing a critical essay, commenting that the assignment revealed the world around them? Deep learning occurs when students have the opportunity to construct new ideas based on prior knowledge and experience with assessment that integrates thinking, feeling, and acting (Bruner, 1966; Kafai & Resnik, 1996; Novak & Gowin, 1984). Students in our Leadership in Aviation course at GU enjoyed constructing their essay. The assignment helped them developed insight and practical skills necessary for future leadership positions. During the writing process, we encouraged effective learning by applying "The Five Rs" to the assessment item.

Making it Work

We contend that the application of The Five Rs—Reason, Reflection, Real World, Rubric, and Realization—to assessment items (such as an essay), offers best practices approach to assessment techniques in tertiary education and enhances the student learning experience in all learning environments.

Why an essay?

A variety of assessment items and methods have emerged in higher education over the past two decades. As an adjunct lecturer, there is little time, guidance, training, or resources to test the applicability of contemporary assessment methods to courses. Thus, lecturers often revert to traditional assessment techniques (e.g., essays). In this course, the essay provided the perfect solution to encourage deeper learning in the achievement of higher order learning objectives.

The major assessment

Our critical essay required students to "use the theory you have learned to explain the leadership component of your personal experiences. You should discuss four events, two of which should be events you experienced personally. The remaining two events should be aviation related and could be drawn from a variety of scholarly and/or media related sources."

We applied The Five Rs to enhance the student learning experience.

What are The Five Rs?

1. **Reason**

   When rationale is hidden, it causes confusion in interpretation for students. Thus, it is crucial that we clearly articulate the purpose of learning (George, 2009). In our course, we clearly linked learning objectives to the assessment question. The learning objective terms such as "analysis of leadership theory," and "apply…to your personal and professional life" were transposed in the assessment question offering a clear link between learning objectives and the assessment. This emphasized the purpose of the assessment and offered students a reason to complete the essay.

2. **Reflection**

Self-**reflection** helps students to validate their understanding of concepts and encourages them to keep abreast of course readings and theories (Walser, 2009). The essay question asked students to **reflect** by considering a personal experience and explaining this experience with respect to the theory they had learned. The activity inspired students to construct knowledge from personal experience and develop techniques to reflect on their own practice as leaders in the aviation industry in the future; essentially scaffolding their knowledge by building on what they already know (Biggs & Tang, 2007).

3. **Real world**

Learning is only significant when the outcomes provide students with **real world** complexities and allow students to understand their future roles in industry (Killen, 2005). After asking students to consider learning from their personal experiences, the essay required students to apply the same process of learning to aviation specific cases. This prepares the students by highlighting the skills necessary for careers in the **real world.**

4. **Rubric**

A **rubric** is a detailed guide to the grading criteria specifying how grades will be applied to the assessment. The use of rubrics is heavily debated in the literature. Some authors argue that rubrics drive students to focus on the 'performance' of the task rather than the 'learning,' thereby failing to provide a sound assessment of a complex student work (Norton, 2009; Sadler, 2008). However, recent research by Malini Redi and Andrade (2010) indicates higher achievement and deeper learning by students who have a **rubric** to guide them. In this course, a detailed rubric supplemented careful explanation to students. By explaining the **rubric**, we offered feedback by helping students understand what was expected of them to achieve the learning objectives and complete the essay successfully.

5. **Realization**

To ensure students understood assessment and outcomes, we required students to perform and submit a self-assessment of their essay against the rubric. This offers three benefits. Engaging in self-assessment: a) encouraged students to **realize** how the marking would be applied; b) encouraged students to **realize** their potential for improvements and address any deficiencies prior to submission; and c) allowed marking

efficiencies for the examiner. In 9 out of 10 cases, student marks were within five percent of the examiner mark with little additional handwritten feedback required.

When we applied the Five Rs to the assessment, the course received much-improved scores on the student course evaluation surveys as compared with previous years. Students commented on their great satisfaction with the course content, learning activities, learning outcomes and assessment feedback.

The activity inspired students to construct knowledge from personal experience.

· · · · · · · · · · ·

Future Implications

To ensure The Five Rs are applied, spend time explaining what is expected of the student. Publishing the question is not enough. Encourage students to meaningfully apply their learning in your course by offering exercises in critical analysis in class. Remember to offer feedback, relating in-class examples to assessment and the grading rubric. This strategy provides an optimum learning experience and encourages the discipline of life-long learning. Our favorite student comment is, "…the assignment has opened my eyes and even changed the way I view people's behaviors in certain situations and [I] can't help but think about those leadership qualities. More so, I think it has enabled me to look at myself and my personal behaviors."

References

Biggs, J., & Tang, C. (2007). *Teaching for quality learning at university*. England, UK: McGraw Hill: Society for Research into Higher Education & Open University Press.

Bruner, J. (1966). *Toward a theory of instruction*. Cambridge, MA: Harvard University Press.

George, J. (2009). Classical curriculum design. *Arts and Humanities in Higher Education, 8*(2), 160–179.

Kafai, Y., & Resnik, M. (1996). *Constructivism in practice: Designing, thinking, and learning in a digital world*. Mahwah, NJ: Lawrence Erlbaum Associates.

Killen, R. (2005). *Programming and assessment for quality teaching and learning*. Victoria, Australia: Thomson Learning.

Malini Redi, Y., & Andrade, H. (2010). A review of rubric use in higher education. *Assessment & Evaluation in Higher Education, 35*(4), 435–448.

Norton, L. (2009). Assessing student learning. In H. Fry, S. Ketteridge & S. Marshall (Eds.), *A handbook for teaching and learning in higher education: Enhancing academic practice.* London & New York: Taylor and Francis Group.

Novak, J., & Gowin, B. (1984). *Learning how to learn.* Cambridge: Cambridge University Press.

Sadler, R. (2008). Indeterminacy in the use of preset criteria for assessment and grading. *Assessment & Evaluation in Higher Education, 34*(2), 159–179

Walser, T. (2009). An action research study of student self-assessment in higher educaion. *Innovative Higher Education, 34*(5), 299–306.

How to Engage Students and Create High Teaching Presence in Online Courses

Janice Poston
Spalding University

Janice Poston, Ed.D., has been an academic librarian for over 20 years and has been teaching as adjunct faculty for 7 years. Since 2006 she has also led the training/coaching efforts for faculty training in course management systems, Blackboard and now Moodle.

Keywords: Teaching Presence, Online Teaching, Hybrid Teaching

Framework

The growing popularity of online and hybrid courses among higher education students is well-documented with 6.7 million students taking at least one online class in 2013 (Allen & Seaman, 2013). The explosive growth of online courses has led to faculty concerns regarding the distance in time and space between students and instructors. Thus, tools and strategies are needed to reduce such distance. As an educator who enjoys teaching face-to-face, just creating a relationship between myself and students in an online format has challenged me to be creative in designing my classes.

The explosive growth of online courses has led to faculty concerns.

Many researchers have examined the relationship between instructors and students throughout the years, but until the last two decades such studies focused on the face-to-face environment (Chickering & Gamson, 1986; Gorham, 1988; Mandermach, Donelli, Dailey, & Schultz, 2005; Mehrabian, 1969; Moore, 1989; Northrup, 2002). Garrison, Anderson, and Archer (2000) postulated that every course has three components: social, content, and teaching. Teaching presence refers to the relationship between students and instructors. Garrison's et al., (2000) model serves as framework to understand the intersection between these three components and its impact on student learning.

Making It Work

One of the primary vehicles used to build teaching presence is that of asynchronous discussion boards or forums; however, faculty are often disappointed with the responses received using such tools. Course design, an element of teaching presence, is of primary importance in assuring responses that are adequate in terms of both quantity and quality (Lemak, Shin, Reed, & Montgomery, 2005).

To improve this situation the author created a series of forums for an introductory university course focused on study skills. The first forum involved students describing themselves, both textually and visually. As part of this assignment students created a visual representation of themselves and their study habits and learning style. The instructor gave clear guidelines for the assignment in both text and podcast format. The instructor answered all e-mails within 24 hours. The visual representation helped students feel a part of a class. Visual representations chosen by the students included pictures of themselves, objects, Post-it notes with adjectives, dolls, toys, a messy work desk, etc. Such representation showed aspects of their personality, such as kindness (e.g., dolls) as well aspects from their work life, such as being overwhelmed with work (e.g., messy desk). Student replies demonstrated that students saw reflections of their personality or life situations in the visual representations uploaded by other students. Other forums required students to share resources that would be helpful to other students, and this forum was also well-received. Replies to this forum demonstrated the usefulness of resources to others pursuing the same goals.

Future Implications

The author shared very clear criteria for forum postings throughout the course. Implications are that forums should be used in online and hybrid courses to increase teaching presence and by increasing such presence successful student outcomes would occur. The frequency, timing, and clarity of responses when using forums is of great importance in determining the outcomes. Additionally, feedback that is both auditory and textual may have even greater impact and its use should be explored (Ice, Curtis, Phillips, & Wells, 2007).

References

Chickering, A. W., & Gamson, Z. F. (1986). Seven principles of good practice in undergraduate education. *AAHE Bulletin*, 39(7), 3–7.

Garrison, D. R., Anderson, T., & Archer, W. (2000). Critical inquiry in a text-based environment: Computer conferencing in higher education. *The Internet and Higher Education*, 2(2–3), 87–105. doi: 10. 1016/ S1096-7516(00)00016-6.

Ice, P., Curtis, R., Phillips, P., & Wells, J. (2007). Using asynchronous audio feedback to enhance teaching presence and students' sense of community. *Journal of the Asynchronous Learning Network*, 11(2), 3–25. Retrieved from http://sloanconsortium.org/jaln/v11n2/using-asyn chronous-audio-feedback-enhance-teaching-presence -and-students%E2%80%99-sense-community.

Lemak, D., Shin, S., Reed, R., & Montgomery, J. (2005). Technology, transactional distance, and instructor effectiveness: An empirical investigation. *Academy of Management Learning & Education*, 4(2), 150–158.

Mandermach, B. J., Donnelli, E., Dailey, A., & Schulte, M. (2005). A faculty evaluation model for online instructors: Mentoring and evaluation in the online classroom. *Online Journal of Distance Learning Administration*, 8(3). Retrieved from http://www.westga.edu/~distance/ojdla /fall83/mandermach83.htm.

Mehrabian, A. (1967). Attitudes inferred from non-immediacy of verbal communication. *Journal of Verbal Learning and Verbal Behavior*, 6(2), 294–295.

Moore, M. G. (1989). Three types of interaction. *The American Journal of Distance Education*, 3(2), 1–6. doi: 10. 1080/08923648909526659.

Northrup, P. T. (2002). Online learners' preferences for interaction. *The Quarterly Review of Distance Education*, 3, 219–226.

Incorporating Seven Principles for Good Practice in Undergraduate Education in Online and Traditional Courses

MIMI O'MALLEY
SPALDING UNIVERSITY

Mimi O'Malley wrote and taught four fully online professional development courses centering on online course delivery and course design for terminally degreed faculty. She currently teaches a traditional multimedia applications course for undergraduate education students.

Keyword: Faculty, Instructional Strategies, Best Practice

In 1987, Arthur Chickering and Zelda Gamson set out to create a statement of principles conducive to an undergraduate education reform movement taking place. Backed by the American Association for Higher Education and the Johnson Foundation, the pair created a document which garnered the 'collective wisdom' drawn from faculty, administrators, state higher education agencies and government policymakers (Chickering & Gamson, 1999, p. 76). *Seven Principles for Good Practice in Undergraduate Education* (1987) is an influential guideline for traditional classroom instruction, yet it is considered best practice for online instruction as well. I will explore how I incorporated these seven principles into the courses I taught for terminally degreed online faculty and pre-service teacher educators.

Good Practice Encourages Student-Faculty Contact. Instructor social presence adds the realization that a human is monitoring the course, even if it is virtually. Scott Miller and Stephen Redman (2010) discovered students who perceived a strong instructor presence had a more positive attitude toward the course. BP501 is an introductory foundation to an online instruction five-week full online course. I added an introductory welcome video summarizing my credentials for teaching BP501. The video also included personal information about me that is not normally included in my CV or resume. Personal information is similar to the experience when traditional students come to their instructor's campus office, scanning the room to see mementoes, diplomas, or family photos.

Good Practice Encourages Cooperation among Students. Clark and Mayer (2003) suggest that one way to build cooperation among students is to design assignments online that require collaboration among learners. BP502 is a five-week fully online course which examines ways that online instructors can incorporate more active learning strategies. Aside from BP502's weekly discussion forum, one module assignment required each student to research an engagement theory (e.g., transactional distance theory) and cite a real-world example of how that theory was put into practice using a Moodle Database activity. Students could make comments on database entries as well as print the entire database list for their own personal reference once the class concluded.

Good Practice Encourages Active Learning. Learning is not a spectator sport according to Chickering and Gamson (1987, p. 1). One think-pair-share assignment in BP502 required students to design an assignment in their discipline for an upcoming online class (e.g., group work project). Another student was paired and assigned to review the assignment based on strengths, weaknesses, and recommendations for deployment. This activity is successful if reviewers are given a rubric which details specific criteria reviewers must examine for greater evaluative feedback.

Good Practice Encourages Prompt Feedback. Seventy-nine percent of the students surveyed expect assignments to be graded immediately, and at the very least within 2 business days, but no later than the following week (Mupinga, Nora, & Yaw, 2006). I created Moodle scoring guides for the five graded, non-automated assignments in BP50 and BP502. I found scoring guides reduced grading time from 5–10 minutes for each assignment in comparison to grading without a scoring guide. I am able to duplicate the scoring guide for successive sections. For future sessions, I plan to switch from Moodle scoring guides to rubrics for all non-automated assignments and discussion forums because

Moodle rubrics may align with outcomes which provide a rigorous course reporting tool.

Good Practice Emphasizes Time on Task. Self-regulation is an important student skill not only during their academic career, but also in their professional/personal lives. Allocating realistic amounts of time benefits both students (effective learning) and faculty (effective instruction)(Chickering & Gamson, 1987). No matter the course, I sent module overviews providing background on upcoming learning outcomes (among other details) each Monday the module opened, using Moodle's News Forum. Conversely, I sent module summaries highlighting key forum posts and upcoming due dates each Friday. These class announcements were gentle reminders that students needed to log into the course regularly while also demonstrating instructor presence.

Good Practice Communicates High Expectations. When students know what is expected of them early in the course, they can focus on ways to best achieve those expectations. Rubrics are a valuable way to convey instructor expectations. Using a knowledge survey to self-assess student present knowledge can also be helpful. I use a 3-point scale (3 = high confidence, 1 = no confidence) to assess student knowledge (Nuhfer, 2009). My EDU379 undergraduate pre-service teachers took a survey at the start of the first module using QuestionPro.com. This survey polled students to rank their experience using nine multimedia applications that I would be addressing over the course of six weeks. With a 50 percent completion rate, the results showed that I would need to provide additional in-class demonstration and exercises for infographics, webquests, and webliographies.

Good Practice Respects Diverse Talents and Ways of Learning. Students often use different combinations of learning modes depending on the learning situations, (Barnes, Preziosi, & Gooden, 2004). Incorporating universal design principles (UDL) into your course assists students with multiple learning styles and abilities. As part of an assignment to create an Instruction Guide, my EDU379 students were required to add alt-text descriptions to all screenshots or images displayed. For future sessions, I would recommend demonstrating how to add captions or transcripts to uploaded YouTube videos.

These principles are foundational for traditional, hybrid, or fully online courses. Addressing these seven principles requires a heightened sense of awareness on the part of the instructor. With a campus initiative to increase UDL awareness, I believe there will be an improved emphasis on creating active learning activities irrespective of the learning abilities for all learners.

References

Barnes, B., Preziosi, R., & Gooden, D. (Spring, 2004). "An examination of the learning styles of online MBA students and their preferred course delivery methods." *New Horizons in Adult Education, 18*(2). Retrieved from, http://www.huizenga.nova.edu/About/ResearchReports/online-MBA-students.cfm

Chickering, A. W., & Gamson, Z. F. (1987). "Seven principles for good practice in undergraduate education." *AAHE Bulletin, 39*(7), 3–7.

Chickering, A. W., & Gamson, Z. F. (1999). Development and adaptations of the seven principles for good practice in undergraduate education. *New Directions For Teaching & Learning, 80*, 75.

Clark, R. C., & Mayer, R. (2003). *E-learning and the science of instruction.* San Francisco: Jossey-Bass Pfeiffer.

Miller, S. T., & Redman, S. L. (2010). Improving instructor presence in an online introductory astronomy course through video demonstrations. *Astronomy Education Review, 9*(1), 010115-1-010115-7. doi:10.3847/AER2009072

Mupinga, D., Nora, R., & Yaw, D. (2006). The learning styles, expectations, and needs of online students. *College Teaching, 54*(1), 185–189. Retrieved from, http://web.simmons.edu/~brady/CE/Reading%202.pdf

Nuhfer, E. (2009). *Knowledge surveys: Being clear, organized, and able to prove it.* Retrieved from, http://www.calstate.edu/itl/newsletter/09-winter.shtml

STRATEGIES FOR ENGAGEMENT IN ONLINE COURSES: ENGAGING WITH THE CONTENT, INSTRUCTOR, AND OTHER STUDENTS

BETH DIETZ-UHLER
MIAMI UNIVERSITY

Beth teaches in the Department of Psychology. Her basic teaching philosophy is that students learn better and enjoy learning more when they think and do rather than listen passively. I also have a strong interest in online distance learning and have been designing and teaching online courses for more than 10 years.

JANET E. HURN
MIAMI UNIVERSITY

Janet is the coordinator of Regional E-Learning Initiatives at Miami University as well as an instructor of Physics. She works with faculty to develop online and hybrid courses.

Keywords: Student Engagement, Online, Hybrid, Quality Matters

Framework

In recent years, there has been an increasing focus on student engagement (e.g., Pike & Kuh, 2009; Porter, 2009). Student engagement occurs when "students make a psychological investment in learning. They try hard to learn what school offers. They take pride not simply in earning the formal indicators of success (grades), but in understanding the material and incorporating or internalizing it in their lives" (Newmann, 1992, pp. 2–3). Research (e.g., Kinzie, 2010; Prince, 2004) strongly suggests that when students are engaged, they tend to perform better. When students are actively engaged in the material, they tend to process it more deeply, which leads to successful retention of the material (e.g., Craik & Lockhart, 1972). In this paper, we describe several ways in which online courses can be designed to promote student engagement. All of these techniques are consistent with Quality Matters Rubric Standards (Quality Matters, 2011) area number 5: Learning Interaction and Engagement.

- 5.2 Learning activities provide opportunities for interaction that support active learning.

Engagement with Content	Engagement with the Instructor	Engagement with Other Students
Listen to the audio introductions	Listen to audio introductions	Respond to classmates' critical thinking answers in discussion board
Engage in the online interactive activities	Watch short, how-to videos	Participate in "Open Discussion" in Learning Management System
Complete mini projects	Read frequent feedback in email and in Learning Management System	Participate in exam review activities
Respond to critical thinking questions in discussion forum	Read "bookend" weekly emails	
	Participate in "Ask the Professor" Discussion in Learning Management System	
	Read and respond to individualized "How's it going?" emails	
	Read and respond to professor's email responses	

Figure 3.1. Summary of Strategies for Student Engagement

- 5.3 The instructor's plan for classroom response time and feedback on assignments is clearly stated.
- 5.4 The requirements for student interaction are clearly articulated.

Consistent with Quality Matters, we have used a number of strategies in our course designs to foster student engagement with the course content, with the instructor, and with other students (see figure 3.1. for a summary of these strategies). Below, we will describe in more detail how these simple course design and implementation strategies can be used to promote student engagement.

Making It Work

Student Engagement with Course Content. To encourage students to engage with the course content, we employ several strategies. In most of our courses, students primarily receive content from a textbook and from videos and interactive activities. One strategy we use is to create short

(no more than five-minute) audio introductions to each module. These introductions involve the instructor talking enthusiastically through four to five PowerPoint slides and presenting a general overview of the module content. We use Knovio (www.knovio.com), which is free and does not require any software for students to download. Additionally, we require students to complete a number of engaging, online, interactive activities. These activities are generally in the form of a game, which most students find to be stimulating (e.g., Davidson, 2011). Many activities of this sort can readily be found online (e.g., Merlot: www.merlot.org) or through textbook publishers (e.g., Pearson's MyStatLab: www.mystatlab.com).

Another strategy we use is to require students to complete a "miniproject" for each module. The miniprojects are designed to require students to apply the material from the text and the interactive activities, relate the material to their own lives, to learn or make use of existing skills such as technology or creative abilities, and to be fun. One example of a miniproject includes writing a letter to your grandparents telling them what you will learn in this course, how it applies to your life and to their lives, and what questions you have about the material. When students apply course material to their own lives, they tend to remember the information better (e.g., Roediger, Gallo, & Geraci, 2002). Another example is for students to create a short video (we suggest they use Screenr or Screencast-O-Matic) explaining the parts of the brain and the nervous system. Other mini projects involve creating posters, public-service brochures, and letters to a newspaper editor.

Student Engagement with Instructor. We employ a number of different strategies to encourage interaction with the instructor. In addition to the audio introductions previously described, we also create short, "how-to" videos (using Screenr or Screencast-O-Matic) to present "Frequently Asked Questions" about the course, to show students how to access feedback in the Collaborative Learning Environment (CLE), or to show students how to use software to create a poster. Like the audio introductions, it is important that students know that it is their instructor's voice they are hearing in the audio. Additionally, for each module, students receive feedback from the instructor on their work. Feedback is given in the course CLE as well as via email. The instructor also sends "bookend" e-mails each week which provide general feedback on the prior module and previews the next module. Typically, the instructor will try to add a sentence or two that is not course related, such as a comment about a sporting event or the weather. We also engage with students in an "Ask the Professor" discussion board in the course CLE. The idea is for students to ask questions about the course, the material, or anything else. Other students can then see the student's questions as well as the instructor's response.

One of the most important strategies that we use is to send personalized "how's it going?" e-mails to students two times per semester. The goal of these e-mails is to let students know that we care about them, which we know is vitally important to student success (e.g., Christophel, 1990; Swan & Richardson, 2003). We estimate that about 90% of students respond to these emails to let us know how the class is going for them and how they are doing in general. Finally, we respond quickly to students' e-mails to us. We hear often in course evaluations that students appreciated our quick responses as it let them know that the instructor cared about them. All of these strategies are employed to achieve the goal of promoting student engagement.

Student Engagement with Other Students. There are three primary mechanisms we use to encourage student engagement with other students. First, students are required to post a response to two other students' critical thinking answers in the CLE discussion board. Students post these responses for all modules, so they are interacting every week with their classmates. Second, there is an "Open Discussion" board in the CLE, which students (and the instructor) can use to post comments or questions about anything. In general, if students do not initiate discussion, then the instructor will. Topics might include queries about favorite movies or books, requests for comments on current events, or a simple query asking how everyone's weekend was spent. Third, for each exam, students are required to complete some type of review and post to the discussion board. The review might take the form of generating questions about the material, creating a concept map, or writing a few paragraphs about how the material across three modules is connected. The "interaction" takes place with the requirement that other students are required to read what students have posted (and yes, students are told that the CLE records, for the instructor, who reads what post).

Future Implications

We have been employing these engagement strategies in our courses for many years as they are consistent with how we design our courses with Quality Matters in mind. How do we know if our students are engaged? Research (e.g., Johnson, 2012) suggests that students are engaged when they exhibit the following behaviors:

- Paying attention
- Taking notes
- Listening
- Asking questions
- Responding to questions
- Reacting
- Reading critically
- Writing to learn, creating, planning, problem solving, discussing, debating, and asking questions
- Performing/presenting, inquiring, exploring, explaining, evaluating, and experimenting
- Interacting with other students, gesturing and moving

Anecdotal evidence suggests that our students are exhibiting many of these behaviors, leading us to believe that they are engaged with the material, the instructor, and other students. For example, students are frequently interacting with other students in the online discussion board, they seem to take pride in the miniprojects for each module, and they typically exceed minimum word counts on projects and critical thinking questions. They also regularly engage via email with the instructor and report that they are enjoying the class and learning.

References

Christophel, D. M. (1990). The relationships among teacher immediacy behaviors, student motivation, and learning. *Communication Education, 39,* 323–340.

Craik, F. I. M., & Lockhart, R. S. (1972). Levels of processing: A framework for memory research. *Journal of Verbal Learning and Verbal Behavior, 11,* 671–684.

Davidson, C. N. (2011). *Now you see it: How the brain science of attention will transform theway we live, work, and learn.* New York: Viking.

Johnson, B. (2012). How do we know when students are engaged? *Edutopia.* Retrieved from:http://www.edutopia.org/blog/student-engagement-definition-ben-johnson.

Kinzie, J. (2010). Student engagement and learning: Experiences that matter. In J. Christensen Hughes and J. Mighty (Eds.), *Taking stock: Research on teaching and learning in higher education* (pp. 1390153). Kingston, Canada: School of Public Policies, Queens University at Kingston.

Newmann, F. (1992). *Student engagement and achievement in American secondary schools.* New York, NY: Teachers College Press.

Quality Matters (2011). Retrieved from: http://www.qmprogram.org/lit-review2011-2013-rubricpdf/download/QM%20Lit%20Review%20for%202011-2013%20Rubric.pdf.

Pike, G. R., & Kuh, G. D. (2009). A typology of student engagement for American colleges and universities, *Research in Higher Education, 46*(2), 185–209.

Prince, M. (2004). Does active learning work? A review of the research. *Journal of Engineering Education, 93*(3), 223–231.

Porter, S. (2009). Institutional structures and student engagement. *Research in Higher Education, 47*(5), 521–558.

Roediger, H. L., III, Gallo, D. A., & Geraci, L. (2002). Processing approaches to cognition: The impetus from the levels-of-processing framework. *Memory, 10,* 319–332.

Swan, K., & Richardson, J. C. (2003). Examining social presence in online courses in relation to students' perceived learning and satisfaction. *Journal of Asynchronous Learning Networks, 7,* 68–82.

||||||||||||||||||||||||||||||||||||||||||||||||||||||||||||||||||||||||||||||||||||||||||||||||||||||||||||||||||||||||||||||||||||||||||||||||||||||||

DOING IT RIGHT THE FIRST TIME: UNIVERSAL DESIGN OF COURSE MATERIALS

ROBIN K. MORGAN
INDIANA UNIVERSITY SOUTHEAST

Robin is currently a professor of psychology and serves as the university director of the Faculty Colloquium on Excellence in Teaching. As a graduate student, she also taught as an adjunct faculty member at a community college.

Keywords: Universal Design, Course Materials, Accommodations

What is universal design? Universal design can be defined as an approach to creating course instruction and materials that benefits all students without the need for adaptation or retrofitting. The student, with a universal design approach, is able to control the method of accessing information, enabling the student to be more self-sufficient by removing barriers to access.

A core concept underlying universal design is anticipating and planning for the diverse needs of students. Universal design, when done correctly, results in course materials that enhance learning for all students, not just those with special needs. Universal design principles can save time for instructors, reduce possible stigma associated with asking for special accommodations, and provide a greater sense of equity and fairness for students in your course.

There are many online resources that can provide you information about incorporating universal design principles into the creation of your course and your course materials (e.g., http://www.acpa.nche.edu/sites/default/files/ctad-a.pdf). I will provide you a few quick tips:

- Provide multiple methods for students to demonstrate understanding of essential course content
- Use a variety of instructional methods when presenting material
  - If using an auditory method, make it visual
    - If using narrated PowerPoint slides, also provide a written script
    - If using recorded lectures, also provide a written script
  - If using a visual method, make it auditory
    - If using an image, add alternative text (alt text)

- ○ If using video clips, provide captions
- ■ Use technology to increase accessibility
  - Put appropriate course content online
  - Put the course syllabus online—before the course begins
    - ○ General tips:
    - ○ Use graphs, charts, drawings, and photos whenever possible to augment text; be sure that all are described in the text
  - Choose fonts carefully—Arial and Helvetica are easier for most people to read
  - Choose font size carefully—small fonts are very difficult to read
  - PDF files may not be accessible; post another format

- When creating any document (syllabus, assignments, etc.), use the word processing formatting tools correctly. This is especially important when creating tables or headings.
- Do not use color to convey meaning
- Be careful about use of color to ensure good color contrast; black text on a white or light background is the most readable
- Avoid patterns or images behind the text as this makes reading the document more difficult.
- In online courses, provide simple, consistent navigation.
- Include an accommodation statement on your course syllabus

‖‖

LIVE TWEETING DOCUMENTARIES IN THE CLASSROOM: ENGAGING STUDENTS AND ENHANCING DISCUSSIONS WITH SOCIAL MEDIA

JIMMY A. YOUNG
CALIFORNIA STATE UNIVERSITY, SAN MARCOS

Jimmy Young was an assistant professor in the department of social work at University of Nebraska at Kearney, 2012–2015, and an adjunct professor at Virginia Commonwealth University before that. He now is with California State University, San Marcos. He teaches social work generalist practice and policy, community, and organizational social work and has presented frequently on the use of social media.

Keywords: Social Media, Twitter, Pedagogy

A recent study from the Pew Center Internet Research Project states that 97% of young adults (aged 18–29) use the Internet in a variety of ways (Fox & Rainie, 2014). Indeed many students are now using the Internet for online courses or to help in completing coursework. Some argue that we need to incorporate the use of technology to disrupt the educational process by infusing new technological methods and digital content into education (Hedberg, 2011). Utilizing social media in and out of the classroom is one way to achieve this and increase students' media literacy, social skills, and allow them to be creative in how they learn. This article focuses on one specific social media application, namely Twitter, and how it was used to enhance classroom discussions during and after viewing a documentary film.

I developed and teach a course entitled Social Media, Digital Activism, and eCitizenship both online and in the traditional face-to-face format. This course is focused on using social media to promote, market, and advocate for nonprofit organizations or causes. Throughout this course I use Twitter to interact with the students and share course content

to engage students through experiential learning methods. Twitter has been used in education in a variety of ways to allow students to extend their learning outside of the classroom and engage in a variety of discussions (Chamberlin & Lehmann, 2011; Elavsky, Mislan, & Elavsky, 2011; Gao, Luo, & Zhang, 2012). Using documentaries in the classroom is nothing new but I found it very beneficial to pair the viewing of a documentary with the assignment of live-tweeting during the film.

Live-tweeting required some preparation, such as how to integrate the course Hashtag (#SOWK388) so tweets could be aggregated into one's message. Twitter only allows for 140 characters and so using a shorter hashtag is best. There are many tutorials and blogs online to help individuals become familiar with Twitter and how to engage in live Twitter chats, such as Teaching Social Work. Additionally, each student used a mobile device to access the Internet and the Twitter website or application during the documentary and this required WiFi in the classroom. I asked students to share any thoughts, reactions, and/or quotes from the documentary as we watched it over the course of two class periods. Even though I figured many students were used to multitasking while they watch TV, I required participation to help keep students engaged in the documentary. I used a third-party application, HootSuite, on my iPad to aggregate all the tweets using the course hashtag and monitor the messages students were sharing during the course of the documentary. I also responded to students on Twitter during the film to help them further explain or express their thoughts and push their critical thinking to a deeper level. At the conclusion of the documentary I held an in-class discussion. I was able to go back to Twitter to draw students into the class discussion by highlighting their tweets and asking them to expand upon their thoughts and comments. This was by far the best in-class discussion of the semester.

The main takeaway for others who may want to adopt this in their course is to think ahead of time to organize the activity. Aggregating the Tweets is simple using HootSuite or some other application. It would be nice to incorporate another screen at the front of the class with a display of the aggregated tweets so students could actively see and communicate with their peers during the film. Additionally, using an archival service such as Storify could help to keep the student's tweets on the web in a space where they could reflect on the messages that were posted during the film. I kept notes during the film that I wanted to further discuss with the class at the end and shared some of the questions via Twitter. Because not all students responded, I used those questions in class and was able to highlight those students who did respond and further engage in a dialogue while encouraging other students to participate. It is also important to have enough class time for the discussion and processing of Twitter messages after the film.

This activity helped to keep students engaged in the documentary and thinking about what was being conveyed because they needed to think critically about how to share their reaction in less than 140 characters of text. I was amazed at the level of attention and critical analysis that students shared in relation to the content of the documentary. I am certain this activity helped students grasp other concepts in the course as they recognized previous learning objectives from earlier in the semester and applied them in the discussion. Additional outcomes from this assignment

included the development of group participation skills, increased cognition, and meta-processing. This occurred because of the need to attend to multiple sources of information and then respond. Students reported that the in-class discussion had the most participation of the semester and that it was helpful to see their tweets because they could remember more clearly what they thought or felt during a specific portion of the film. Future research will be centered on evaluating course objectives and learning outcomes more directly with the use of a rigorous design. One simple way of accomplishing this will be to poll students via Twitter after the discussion.

Live-tweeting documentaries may not work for every class, because not every class is equipped with the technology. With some creative planning and the Internet, students can begin to use Twitter to live-tweet during any film that is shown in or out of class. By doing so, students will be able to increase their media literacies, think critically and creatively, and engage in the course content in a manner that they will be sure to remember.

References

Chamberlin, L., & Lehmann, K. (2011). Twitter in higher education. In C. Wankel (Ed.), *Educating educators with social media (cutting-edge technologies in higher education, Volume 1)* (pp. 375–391). United Kingdom: Emerald Group Publishing Limited.

Elavsky, C .M., Mislan, C., & Elavsky, S. (2011). When talking less is more: Exploring outcomes of Twitter usage in the large-lecture hall. *Learning, Media and Technology, 36*(3), 215–233. doi: 10.1080/17439884.2010.549828

Gao, F., Luo, T., & Zhang, K. (2012). Tweeting for learning: A critical analysis of research on microblogging in education published in 2008–2011. *British Journal of Educational Technology, 43*(5), 783–801. doi: 10.1111/j.1467-8535.2012.01357.x

Hedberg, J. G. (2011). Towards a disruptive pedagogy: Changing classroom practice with technologies and digital content. *Educational Media International, 48*(1), 1–16.

Richardson, W. H. (2006). *Blogs, wikis, podcasts, and other powerful web tools for classrooms.* Thousand Oaks, CA: Corwin Press.

With some creative planning and the Internet, students can begin to use Twitter to live-tweet during any film that is shown in or out of class.

MULTIPLE LEARNING ENVIRONMENTS IN HIGHER EDUCATION

ASHLEY HASTY
INDIANA UNIVERSITY

Dr. Hasty has taught merchandising as a lecturer for 3 years.

Keywords: High-Impact, Environments, Engagement

Framework

Studies indicate that deep learning typically occurs outside the classroom, and high-impact learning activities identified by students through the National Survey of Student Engagement (NSSE) are also occurring outside the classroom; these include internships, study abroad, research, and capstone projects (Young, 2011). Another study indicates "that active learning increases examination performance by just less than half a standard deviation and that lecturing increases failure rates by 55%." (Freeman et al., 2014) In Teaching Naked, the author suggests we "abandon campus class time entirely" and move the learning process to labs, studios, sites of internships, civic engagement, or study abroad (Bowen, 2012). Clearly we need to rethink the environments in which learning occurs and the methods with which students are taught.

Making it Work

The NSSE offers a framework for alternative learning environments with potential to facilitate deep learning through high-impact, student-faculty interactions. Internships and civic engagement are the first high-impact learning activities listed by the NSSE and Bowen. "Internship programs engage students in service activities primarily for the purpose of providing students with hands-on experiences that enhance their learning or understanding of issues relevant to a particular area of study" (Figure 3.2. Furco, 2000). Apparel merchandising students in my course create visual

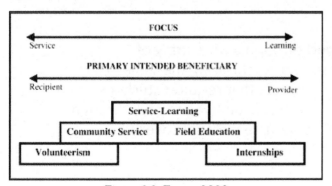

Figure 3.2. Furco, 2000

displays of merchandise for four community sites in an internship-like learning environment. First, they contact the community agency to identify the agency's needs and desires for the visual display and later design and implement that display at the agency location. I prefer to call this activity service-learning because the students' service to the four agencies "equally benefit the provider and the recipient of the service" (Furco, 2000). This opportunity provides students with a real-life, hands-on example of what visual merchandisers do. It requires students to use the content they used in class while delivering a product that satisfies the community site.

During the regular academic year, I am unable to provide students with a true study-abroad experience. However, according to one study, study-abroad participants "reported that studying abroad enabled them to tolerate ambiguity... and to learn something about themselves..." (Dwyer, 2004). These, of course, are among many benefits associated with the study-abroad experience. I developed a series of field trip experiences with corresponding lessons that introduce ambiguity requiring reflection. I organized these field trips so that those with the most ambiguous relationships with visual merchandising (the art museum, cultural museum, and greenhouse) occur in the first third of the course and those with direct relationships with visual merchandising (downtown shopping area, shopping mall, and stand-alone retail stores) occur in the second third of the course. Examples of prompts are provided below:

- How have two retail stores in similar shopping environments (such as two stores in a mall or two stores in a downtown shopping area) approached a similar merchandise display challenge with different outcomes?
- Connect this learning experience to previous experiences (working in groups, working with the community, working at a job, other class assignments, etc.)
- What personal qualities have you developed through service-learning? In what ways do you anticipate these qualities will help you in the future?
- How did our in-class activities guide, direct, or influence your design decisions at your service site?

By taking students to a variety of learning environments, I am able to provide real-life, concrete examples of course topics. In addition, I am able to illustrate how visual merchandising skills can be used in a variety of ways.

I introduce the cumulative capstone project after all field trip experiences are complete. Classes during this final third of the semester resemble a studio-style course. Students come to class prepared to work on their project while receiving feedback from me each day. The capstone project is either an industry-designed case study, a joint project with a class from another field of study (e.g., interior design), or is created anew by me—all of these options share a substantial research requirement. This organization allows adjustment of lessons in the first two-thirds of the class to better fit whichever capstone is being used in a given semester. It also ensures the inclusion of fresh material in the course, preventing curricular stagnancy.

In the industry-designed case study, students were required to design new fixtures, presentations, and floor plans for a Sephora store. This required students to research beauty supply companies to determine how products were currently being displayed at Sephora and competing stores. It also required students to research how other types of merchandise are displayed in innovative ways (e.g., could a beauty store learn a presentation technique from an electronics store?) Students investigate trends in fixtures to generate new ideas for fixtures that could be used in their Sephora presentation. Finally, students researched how customers shop in beauty supply stores, the Sephora customer profile, and determined which products are important to this customer.

In summary, students are engaged through a wide array of learning environments, progressively less abstract during the semester. Students are prompted to critically reflect on these experiences in a variety of ways (short and long form, public and private). The course culminates with a capstone project that requires students to merge the aforementioned experiences with substantive research through a comprehensive application of all the course material covered.

Future Implications

Multiple learning environments are most effective in small class sizes. I originally taught this class to 30 students, subsequently reducing the course size to 24. Learning environments and the associated assignments are also modified each semester. I can see any field of study being able to apply the multiple learning environments model. Rather than talking in the abstract inside the classroom, take students into the community to show them exactly what you are talking about.

References

Barnett, R. (2010). *Being a university (foundations and futures of education)*. New York City: Routledge.

Bowen, J. A. (2012). *Teaching naked: How moving technology out of your college classroom will improve student learning*. San Francisco: Jossey-Bass.

Dwyer, M. M. (2004). Charting the impact of studying abroad. *International Educator*, 14–17, 19–20.

Freeman, S., Eddy, S., McDonough, M., Smith, M. K., Okoroafor, N., Jordt, H., et al. (2014). Active learning increases student performance in science, engineering, and mathematics. *Proceedings of the National Academy of Sciences of the United States of America*, 1–6.

Furco, A. (2000). Service-learning: A balanced approach to experiential education. *In Introduction to Service-Learning Toolkit*, Providence, RI: Campus Compact.

Young, J. R. (2011). Actually going to class, for a specific course? How 20th-century new learning technologies prompt a rethinking of traditional course structure. *Chronicle of Higher Education*, A14.

In summary, students are engaged through a wide array of learning environments, progressively less abstract during the semester. The course culminates with a capstone project that requires students to merge the aforementioned experiences with substantive research through a comprehensive application of all the course material covered.

LEADING CLASSROOM DISCUSSIONS

ROBIN K. MORGAN
INDIANA UNIVERSITY SOUTHEAST

Robin is currently a professor of psychology and serves as the university director of the Faculty Colloquium on Excellence in Teaching. As a graduate student, she also taught as an adjunct faculty member at a community college.

KIMBERLY T. OLIVARES
INDIANA UNIVERSITY

Kimberly holds a MA in Student Affairs and Higher Education. She joined IU as an academic advisor and waded into the forum of teaching freshman seminars and Organizational Behavior as an adjunct. She currently works to support the teaching mission of IU on all eight of its campuses with FACET.

Keywords: Discussion, Engagement

Framework

For students, a poorly designed classroom discussion becomes no more than expressing opinions. At worst, classroom discussions can devolve into pockets of students expressing their opinions—with no supporting facts—while other students sit with glazed eyes or read their messages on their cell phones. A well-constructed and well-facilitated classroom discussion can provide students wonderful learning opportunities and to the instructor an opportunity to engage with students, encouraging critical thinking and inquiry.

Making it Work

Here are a few tips and tricks we have picked up:

- Open-ended questions are vital to classroom discussion. Don't ask yes or no questions.
- Give students time to form a coherent response. These silent seconds seem to last forever when you are at the front of the classroom but they truly are only seconds. The silence will end and someone will respond. We promise!
- Don't answer your own question; for example, "I think Freud was a freak, what do you think?" A better way to go about this would be to ask students, "What do you think of Freud's concept of the Oedipus complex?"
- Prepare for classroom discussion. This isn't something that most instructors can do on the fly. Determine where you want the discussion to go—what concepts or ideas do you want on the discussion to address and how will students be led to those concepts or ideas? What leading questions can you pose?

- Learning student names and calling on students (even timid ones) is important. You can use a variety of methods to call on students. Whatever method you use should ensure that the same students are not always talking. Be sure to include as many students as possible and use a process that allows for some unpredictability.
- We also encourage you to break your class into smaller groups so they can discuss topics with peers. You can mingle among the groups and try to synthesize the information when you bring the whole class back together. When using smaller groups, be sure to find a simple method to assign small groups that doesn't eat up class time. In addition, provide instructions before allowing students to move to their small groups. Finally, be sure to always leave time for each group to report back to the class as a whole.

Creating and leading discussions will get easier.

Future Implications

As you become more comfortable, creating and leading discussions will get easier. You will also be able to better anticipate which concepts may lead to better discussions. We encourage you to get to know your students personally and build a community of learning in your classrooms so students feel open to sharing their ideas and questions.

MODELING A LEARNING COMMUNITY FOR FUTURE SECONDARY TEACHERS

LUCY GUEVARA-VÉLEZ
WESTERN MICHIGAN UNIVERSITY

Lucy has taught as an adjunct instructor for the Department of Teaching, Learning, and Educational Studies at Western Michigan University since 2013.

Keywords: Learning Community, Pre-Service Teachers

Framework

Teaching is the one profession that has been modeled for us on a daily basis since early childhood. As we get older, we begin to create a list of the teachers we loved and respected. This means that those of us who want to be teachers enter college with preconceived ideas of teaching. Each semester, the pre-service teachers in my introductory course are asked to reflect upon their own educational journeys, and their narratives reveal one thing: the executive approach to teaching, an approach that can be traced back to the early 1900s, remains popular in 2014 (Fenstermacher & Soltis, 2009). Most importantly, these students identify its management driven focus as great teaching. They are eager to learn how to control, discipline, or fix the student. My course in a way, offers an opportunity to force a shift in paradigm, and prepare future teachers who engage in building and empowering communities.

This Quick Hit provides suggestions to help model a learning community in teacher preparation courses. This pedagogical design is not new. It is rooted in the work of John Dewey during the 1920s and found its way into undergraduate education in the 1970s (Shapiro & Levine, 1999). The following tips explain basic strategies that can turn your course into a learning community. Although any course can be transformed into a learning community, it is especially important for future teachers to experience this type of educational setting.

Making It Work

Syllabus & Course Design
First, I consider the syllabus to be a contract—a document that outlines the course design, its goals, required texts, assignments, grading, and expectations. It also addresses the course's commitment to community, not only the learning community that you will be creating during a specific semester but the community that these young adults will impact as they graduate college. In addition, the syllabus should clearly show the framework for your course. In my

case, it emphasizes the relevance of critical pedagogy and social justice in education. Students are aware from day one that the course is not the typical "sit and listen" class. They will be expected to collaborate with peers and our end goal is social consciousness. My personal position is transparent and written in the syllabus, because teaching is not business … it's personal. Don't forget to include attendance goals, the guidelines for missed assignments, as well as, any university policies. These regulations create clear expectations that help support your learning community.

Instruction & Collaboration
Second, teaching strategies must complement the learning community. For my course, I develop activities according to the assigned readings or the topics to be discussed. I use multiple forms of instruction such as short lectures, individual presentations, small group collaborations, and class discussions. Lectures are interactive and push students to actively engage by talking, listening, and exchanging feedback. Students' voices become part of the curriculum. Students assume active roles as discussants, contributors, collaborators, and problem solvers. For example, in my class, students work together to present a specific reading, discuss a current issue in public education, and even formulate questions for the midterm or final exams. This makes students active agents in their own learning. Within a learning community, the instructor no longer represents power. We serve a new function as facilitators, collaborators, and co-learners. I rearrange tables and chairs to resemble a U shape and this further de-centers my role as instructor, allows for collaboration, and prompts students to listen to each other. The focus is our community.

Assignments & Assessments
Third, readings and assignments provide students with a wide range of opportunities to explore the teaching profession and demonstrate their own personal and academic strengths. For example, the use of narrative or ethnographic texts allows future teachers to gain knowledge from primary sources. Most importantly, these texts refute generalizations and deconstruct deficit notions of teaching, students,

parents, and communities. Using meaningful texts is an engaging way to help future teachers understand diversity (Carger, 2005). This type of class exercise also motivates them to articulate their own narratives, listen to others, and open up to collaborative learning. Assessments may include multiple forms of activities such as writing assignments, presentations, digital stories, ethnographic projects, podcasts, blogs, and exams.

Rubrics help provide clear instructions and expectations. Exams are stressful for everyone, and many will argue that they are counterproductive in a learning community. Yet, I think that well-written exams can offer students another opportunity to excel. Exams can target different skills that are sometimes overlooked in class. Finally, make time for peer assessments. This not only fosters community but also prepares future teachers for a profession that centers on accountability.

Student-Instructor Relationship & Mentorship

Last, but most important, a respectful and mutual exchange between instructors and students is the foundation for a learning community. I suggest that every instructor who teaches pre-service teachers keep the following eight concepts in mind when shaping learning communities and relationships with students: honesty, responsiveness, respect, openness, empowerment, collaboration, trust, and challenge (Cox, 2002). You can ensure a strong relationship with your students if you embrace a teaching philosophy that is humanizing, asset-based, and student centered. In more practical terms, you build trust by: having honest conversations, replying to emails, adjusting the calendar if necessary, making accommodations for students with health or personal issues, and reaching out. We are mentors and must take time to encourage students to seek help on campus if they need it, to engage in community efforts, and even to pursue graduate studies. We must help them develop college-going literacy and make sure they persist and succeed in college.

Future Implications

It is our responsibility, as college instructors, to prepare future teachers who are creatively engaged in building communities. In my experience, this instructional setting builds a sense of community and erases the marginalization that many students feel on big campuses.

One thing that I learned would make this teaching strategy even more successful is to remind students to take notes. Many students have not experienced this instructional setting before, and require our help to understand that it is still a college course. I've gathered mid-semester, and end-of-semester, student surveys that describe my course as "fun, eye-opening, inclusive, worthwhile, different way of teaching, conducive to discussion, and student-centered."

References

Cox, M. D. (2002). The role of community in learning: Making connections in your classroom and campus, your student and colleagues. In G. S. Wheeler (Ed.), *Teaching and learning in college* (pp.1–38). Elyria, OH: Info Tec.

Carger, C. L. (2005). The art of narrative inquiry: Embracing emotion and seeing transformation. In Phillion, J., Ming, F. H., & Connelly, F. M. (Eds.), *Narrative & experience in multicultural education* (pp. 231–246). Thousand Oaks, CA: Sage Publications.

Fenstermacher, G. D., & Soltis, J. F. (2009). *Approaches to teaching.* New York, NY: Teachers College Press.

Gildersleeve, R. E. (2010). *Fracturing opportunity: Mexican migrant students and college-going literacy.* New York, NY: Peter Lang Publishing.

Shapiro, N. S., & Levine, J. H. (1999). *Creating learning communities: A practical guide to winning support, organizing for change, and implementing programs.* San Francisco, CA: Jossey-Bass Publishers.

Rubrics help provide clear instructions and expectations. Exams are stressful for everyone, and many will argue that they are counterproductive in a learning community. Exams can target different skills that are sometimes overlooked in class.

TURN GRADING INTO A LEARNING OPPORTUNITY

SAYONITA GHOSH HAJRA
UNIVERSITY OF GEORGIA

Sayonita has taught mathematics for the past 7 years. She has taught Calculus, Precalculus, Differential Equations, and Mathematics content courses for elementary teachers as an instructor of record at the University of Georgia.

Keywords: Self-Reflection, Test, Self-Grading, Grading

Framework

As an instructor, how many times did we witness students putting their test paper away or throwing them away after looking at the grade? It is a challenge for instructors to hold the attention of students while reading the answers on the test papers after they are graded.

One can use self-reflection by letting students grade their own test. This helps students to be aware of their own mistakes. I have used this method to grade tests in one of the mathematics content courses for future teachers.

Making It Work

Students take a test and the instructor photocopies the students' test paper. In the next class meeting, the instructor returns students' photocopied test paper with a copy of the test's answer key. Students grade their own test paper, using the rubric shown in Figure 3.3. In addition, students give reasons for their grading. For instance, if there is a conflict in grading based on the answer key, students provide their reasoning for their confusion and argue why they are correct.

The instructor grades the students' work and provides a score. The student's grade can be used as extra credit. I found this method of grading to be very effective. This method gives a sense of the students' understanding of the concepts and helps the students to understand where their argument is flawed. Critiquing their own test paper helps students to rethink about the topic and the answers in a deeper way.

Future Implications

This technique can be used in courses other than mathematics. I would like to improve this method by returning test papers to students after the test using an online platform. Students will get 24 hours to grade their own work. This will allow the instructor to provide feedback to students within 48 hours of testing.

	Needs improvement (0.25)	Good (1.25)	Very good (2)	Value
Problem solving	Demonstrate little or no understanding of the problem	Demonstrate a partially correct strategy	Demonstrate a correct strategy	
Reasoning and proof	No correct reasoning or justification provided	Some correct reasoning or justification provided	A correct reasoning and justification provided	
Connections of solutions to problems and concepts	No or little connections	Limited connections	Accurate connections	
Writing presentation	No logical sequencing	Some logical sequencing	Logical sequencing	
Mathematical vocabulary	No use of mathematical vocabulary	Some mathematical vocabularies present without correct use	Use of correct mathematical vocabularies	

Figure 3.3. Grading rubric. This rubric is based on a 10-point scale.

ARE STUDENT LEARNING OUTCOMES REALLY NECESSARY?

ROBIN K. MORGAN
INDIANA UNIVERSITY SOUTHEAST

Robin is currently a professor of psychology and serves as the university director of the Faculty Colloquium on Excellence in Teaching. As a graduate student, she also taught as an adjunct faculty member at a community college.

Keywords: Learning Outcomes, Assessment, Objectives

Over the past decade, a faculty member in academia would need to have been living under a rock to miss the introduction of student learning outcomes (SLOs). SLOs have quickly become a 'best practice' in higher education and for accrediting bodies. However, do SLOs really have any impact on student learning?

By SLOs (also referred to as student learning objectives), I am discussing faculty-created statements detailing what students are expected to demonstrate as a result of completing a course. That is, what do I, as the instructor, expect my students to learn in this course? SLOs are written in measurable terms with active verbs identifying what students should be able to demonstrate, represent, or produce. That is, a SLO such as "students will appreciate the benefits of science" would not be as measurable as a SLO that states "students will compare and contrast major theories in the field." Bloom's taxonomy (1984) has been useful in helping faculty to create SLOs that focus on overt behavior that can be measured.

Much time and attention has been paid to helping faculty develop these SLOs and incorporating them into syllabi and assessment plans. From an instructor's perspective, is this time worthwhile? That is, do SLOs enhance student learning?

SLOs provide a description of what you are trying to accomplish. They focus on what the students will learn, rather than on how you will structure their learning. When I provide students the SLO, "students will compare and contrast major theories in the field," students have a good understanding of what I expect them to be able to do to be successful in my course. Of course, as an instructor, this means that **I must align my course assessments (assignments, quizzes, exams) to match my SLOs.**

SLOs can also help me, as an instructor, to determine when students are not successful. By helping to **create a feedback loop**, it is easier for me to assess my own effectiveness as an instructor and to identify those areas that need to be revised.

In the final analysis, without explicit and measurable SLOs, I would argue that we have little evidence that what we are doing enhances student learning. SLOs allow us to create a culture of evidence when it comes to teaching. Such a culture has the long-term advantage of enhancing student learning and increasing the value of what we do in our classrooms.

Reference

Bloom, B. S. (1984). *Taxonomy of educational objectives: Book 1: Cognitive domain*. London, England: Longman.

SLOs can also help me, as an instructor, to determine when students are not successful. By helping to create a feedback loop, it is easier for me to assess my own effectiveness as an instructor and to identify those areas that need to be revised.

Using Project-Based Service-Learning as Text for Reflection

Ashley Hasty
Indiana University

Dr. Hasty has taught merchandising as a lecturer for 3 years.

Keywords: Service-Learning, Projects, Reflection

Framework

For the three years I taught a service-learning class, I struggled with how to grade the service-learning work. In groups, students enrolled in Strategies in Retail Promotion, an elective for Apparel Merchandising majors, and they complete four merchandise displays for four different community partners. At first I graded the visual display itself. How well did the students apply the visual merchandising concepts to create their visual display? I realized that students might be able to create beautiful displays and still not understand visual merchandising concepts. In the end, I decided to use their projects as "text" for their reflections. Just as a student might write a summary or an analysis of books and articles they read, my students use their experience creating visual displays to write a summary and analysis of their work. Students who read a textbook are not graded for how well they read the text and my students are not graded on how well they completed their projects. Instead, they are graded solely on how well they reflect on their experience. Although using direct-service as a "text" for reflection is not new, I have not yet seen it done in a project-based service-learning course.

Making it Work

My class of 24 students is divided into 8 equal groups of 3. Every two weeks, four of those groups go to our four community partners to create visual displays. At the end of the semester, every student will have completed a visual display for each of our four community partners.

After completing each visual display, students answer the following questions individually:

- **Course-Focused Questions**
  - How did our in-class activities (tours, field trips, in-class worksheets, etc.) guide, direct or influence your design decisions at your service site?
  - Explain how your display is appropriate for your service site brand and target market.
  - Describe your display in terms of design principles and principles of design.
- **Self-Focused Questions**

- Compare your experience at the service site with your previous experiences such as jobs, working in groups, volunteering in the community, or other class assignments.
- What personal qualities have you developed through service-learning? In what ways do you anticipate these qualities will help you in the future?

Students are graded on their answers to the course-focused questions, which tie directly to our course goals. Students are loosely graded (mostly on completion) on the self-focused questions, which are designed to get students to take an active role in their learning.

By grading students on their reflections after the project, I ensure that students didn't just "get lucky" with a strong visual display. Their reflections prove that they understood the concepts and applied them strategically in their project. This also allows me to grade a group project individually, which eliminates free-loaders.

Future Implications

Using a project-based service-learning assignment as "text" could be used for any service-learning course. Grading individual written assignments works best, time-wise, for smaller courses. My course started with 30 students and over time I reduced the cap to 24 students. Many professors of larger classes use project-based service-learning in their courses and they may choose to have the reflection completed as a group if they so desire. I found this grading method to reduce the number of complaints and arguments from students concerning their grade. They see this method as less subjective and I am able to get a clearer sense of what concepts they really know and understand.

I struggled
with how
to grade
the service-
learning work.

• • • • • • • • • • •

Active Learning Strategies

Robin K. Morgan
Indiana University Southeast

Robin is currently a professor of psychology and serves as the university director of the Faculty Colloquium on Excellence in Teaching. As a graduate student, she also taught as an adjunct faculty member at a community college.

Kimberly T. Olivares
Indiana University

Kimberly holds a MA in Student Affairs and Higher Education. She joined IU as an academic advisor and waded into the forum of teaching freshman seminars and Organizational Behavior as an adjunct. She currently works to support the teaching mission of IU on all eight of its campuses with FACET.

Keywords: Active Learning, Strategies, Collaboration

Framework

Active Learning is yet another higher education buzzword —the technique is nothing new or particularly cutting edge other than we now have something to call it when we engage students in their learning process rather than just dispensing our content knowledge directly into their heads (which, let's be honest—doesn't work). Active Learning can involve any of a host of tools you use to engage students with the material, assist students in learning to think critically, and helping students apply the material to their everyday life. These techniques are student or learner centered rather than instructor centered.

Making it Work

You can google 'Active Learning Strategies' and get a plethora of ideas. We have employed some of those ideas in our classrooms and are happy to share our experiences.

In the beginning of the semester, you can use an icebreaker as an active learning strategy (we bet you already do this). Icebreakers get the students moving, engaged in an activity (building community, getting to know each other) and forces them to engage with one another. The selection of the icebreaker is critically important. Icebreakers should be either related to the content of your course or related to future activities that you will require of students. For example, when

> **Techniques are student or learner centered rather than instructor centered.**
> • • • • • • • • • • •

teaching abnormal psychology, I frequently use a myth quiz relating to abnormal psychology. Students complete the quiz individually and then discuss their quiz answers in small groups. I use many group activities so students learn from the first day that I value their participation.

Throughout the semester, and even multiple times in each class session, you can break from lecturing and engage in one or several strategies. Perhaps, a Think-Pair-Share—this gives students a chance to explain what they know to a partner, or respond to a question. They do this first on an individual level, then with a partner, then with the larger class as you ask some groups to share.

If you are in a discipline where it makes sense to use case studies, this technique provides a great way to engage the students with the complexities of applying their knowledge in a real-world setting.

One-minute papers have been used for millennia it seems. In this technique, students are provided one minute to respond to the material from class. The student might write about the one thing they will take away from today's lecture/class, the muddiest point (a point of confusion), what they liked best/worst, etc. One-minute papers are useful for students to assess their own learning as well as potentially useful in identifying the material that a faculty member may need to spend more time explaining in a future class.

Future Implications

As we stated, a quick Google search will provide you with many options and suggestions for active learning strategies. Try some out in your class; there is one or two that you are likely already using or can modify to add to your repertoire.

PROOF OF TECHNOLOGY AS A MULTIPLYING FACTOR IN MACROECONOMIC GROWTH & PRODUCTION

JIM ROGERS
INDIANA UNIVERSITY SOUTH BEND

Jim Rogers has been teaching introductory microeconomics and macroeconomics at Indiana University South Bend as an adjunct professor of Economics at the Judd Leighton School for Business and Economics since 2012.

Keywords: Macroeconomics, Production, Growth, Productivity, Technology, In-Class, Experiment

Framework

Conceptual learning often lacks direct real-world examples or experiences. This full in-class participation experiment allows all students to participate and experience technology as a real-world difference maker in productivity and growth by assigning different, randomly selected, groups as countries with differing levels of technology. Further, it allows them to experience this differential in a sound, socially scientific manner holding relatively constant the other factors of production.

In macroeconomics, technology as a multiplying force for production and growth is a difficult concept for students to grasp. However, demonstrating the power of technology as a multiplier in macroeconomic production and growth can be accomplished through a full involvement, in-class experiment. This in-class experiment accounts for the constants of labor, human capital, capital, and natural resources while isolating for employment of technology using a simple addition problem. The formal macroeconomic equation is expressed as:

$$Y \text{ (production)} = A \text{ (technology)} \times F \text{ (factors of production)}$$
$$(\text{Labor} + \text{Human Capital} + \text{Capital} + \text{Natural Resources})$$

Making It Work

Practical Application of Experiment
- Divide the students into three groups, having them randomly count off one-two-three.
- As they count off begin writing random numbers on the board as an addition problem.
- When they have finished counting off step away from the addition problem on the board.
- Assign the ones to add up the numbers on the board without a calculator or pencil and paper (just in their heads). Assign the twos to use only pencil and paper, no calculator. Assign the threes to use only their calculators.

- Instruct the students to raise their hands as each individual arrives at the answer and announce which group number they represent. Invariably almost all the first done are the threes. Continue conducting the experiment until the twos answer. Then stop the experiment and point out that none of the ones have finished.

Explain that when calculating production and growth in this experiment the number of people in each labor force is roughly the same, the human capital (education level) is roughly the same (as they are all college students in the same course), the capital is the same (as they all are sitting in the same room), on the same chairs with similar vantage points to view the addition problem on the board and that natural resources do not come into play. Therefore, the only real difference is that the technology difference used in the experiment has made the three group multiple times more productive than those in group two and group one.

Future Implications

To further quantify the experiment, you could examine the productivity of each group by timing the total length of time that it took to complete the addition problem and then evaluate how many of these addition problems could be completed in an hour. To do this, take the time required to complete the first problem by each group, divide by the number of people in the group, and then divide that into an hour. This would be valuable for the students to understand as productivity in macroeconomics is universally measured as per capita per hour.

At the conclusion of the experiment, to assess added understanding and achievement of the student learning objective, students are asked to raise their hand if this experiment helped them understand the concept of technology as a multiplying force in production and growth. With no exceptions, all students raise their hand.

Using Quality Matters (QM) to Improve All Courses

Diane L. Finley
Prince George's Community College

Dr. Finley teaches psychology at Prince George's Community College. She stresses the importance of using psychology in the daily lives of her students.

Keywords: Quality Matters, Online Teaching, Hybrid

Framework

Quality Matters is a program of quality assurance for online and hybrid education. The program has received national recognition for its process which includes peer review, faculty-centeredness and a focus on continuous improvement in online teaching and learning. Quality Matters is a subscription program whose current subscribers include community and technical colleges and universities in the United States, other countries, K-12, and other academic institutions. It is a systematic process for ensuring quality in the design of online and blended/hybrid courses and its rubric standards align with accreditation standards. Using Quality Matters also has implications for improving student outcomes and retention. I became involved with QM at its inception in 2003 since I worked at one of the original institutions involved with its development under a Fund for the Improvement of Post-Secondary Education (FIPSE) grant. I eventually became a certified peer reviewer, a certified master reviewer and now I help to train master reviewers. While not entirely sold on the process at first, I witnessed the improvements in my online courses once I applied the rubric to my courses. Students had fewer procedural questions, navigation was smoother, and I was able to focus more on interacting with the students. I became a believer in the rubric and the process.

Making It Work

Before discussing how I specifically use QM in my courses, let me give a bit of background on QM and some specifics about the process. QM was a collaboration of 14 community colleges, 5 four-year institutions in Maryland, and nine external partners. The goal of the FIPSE project was to develop criteria (in a rubric) for quality assurance of online learning and to create training for online faculty. The rubric focused on course design, not delivery, and was not intended to resolve all quality issues in online classes. After the grant

expired, QM became an independent subscriber-based organization under MarylandOnline. Subscribers include educational institutions of all levels as well as publishers of online courses. QM also offers online training for instructors and has to date, trained over 16,000 faculty and instructional design staff. The QM process which is researched-based involves a faculty-centered, peer-review process of online and hybrid (blended) courses. The rubric, now in its third iteration (since becoming a non-profit organization), focuses on course design and is a diagnostic instrument which faculty can use for continuous improvement of their courses. The expectation is that all courses can eventually meet QM expectations. Meeting QM expectations involves meeting the 21 essential standards and receiving at least 85% of the possible points from the rubric. If a course does not initially meet expectation, the faculty member is encouraged to use the feedback from the review to improve the course which is then re-reviewed. The rubric focuses on eight areas: overview, objectives, assessment, materials, learner interaction, technology, learner support, and accessibility. Why worry about course design? Why use Quality Matters? Since the Department of Education changed the rules for federal financial aid in 2005 with the Higher Education Reconciliation Act of 2005 (HERA), the number of institutions offering online courses has increased dramatically. The Sloan Consortium reported a 10% growth in distance learning enrollments in 2011. The Instructional Technology Council which examined elearning at community colleges reported an 8.2% increase in online enrollments from fall 2010 to fall 2011. I now use the QM rubric in all my course designs, even for courses that have not been officially reviewed. As our institution has increased emphasis on assessment, I find using the rubric forces me to see how my course and chapter objectives align with my assessments and activities. Everything in the course has a purpose and that purpose is made clear and transparent to students. Students who read all of the objectives and explanations understand why they are doing particular activities or taking certain quizzes. Applying the rubric has made me really examine my choice of activities and assessments. They are much more purposeful now. Even weekly discussion boards link to specific objectives. I give students a course map that clearly shows this linkage. The research shows that better student outcomes result when a course design relates to the course objectives (Swan, Matthews, Bogle, Boles, & Day, 2011). It was a "duh!" moment when I looked at these rubric standards and the research. Students are also more satisfied when all the course components are clearly integrated (Ke & Xie, 2009).

The rubric has also helped me to make my courses more accessible to all students. I used to use all sorts of font style and colors, not realizing how difficult those can be for some students. Now my courses are more simple in design but they are easier to read. I recently had a visually impaired student who was able to use a screen reader in the course with no problems. The third area in which I have found the rubric most helpful is the Course Overview and Introduction (QM Standard 1). To meet the specific review standards in this area, I created "Start Here" areas for students with detailed directions on how to get started. I include information on my expectations and institutional policies relevant to online learners. I also include links to institutional tutorials on using our LMS. No longer do I assume students can just find these items. I have streamlined my navigation so there are fewer buttons. Students have to click fewer times to find course components. It does take a good deal of time before the course begins to create the designs that meet QM expectations. However, I found that once I completed one course and it met expectations, other courses took less time. There were many items that could be reused with slight edits such as the Start Here sections. I also found that by using the rubric for the design, I was better able to focus on content. Some faculty raise concerns about QM creating packaged courses with no room for individual teaching styles. I have reviewed over 90 courses from all types of institutions. I have not found anything that would resemble a "packaged" course. There are many design elements that can

> The rubric has also helped me to make my courses more accessible to all students... my courses are more simple in design.

> •••••••••••

meet QM expectations. It does not tell any instructor how to teach a class. I have reviewed multiple classes on the same topic and have yet to find two that are just alike, even at the same institution. As mentioned above, by using the QM rubric to guide course design, the faculty member is free to focus on content and devising creative ways of presenting that content to students.

Future Implications

As the body of research literature on online courses continues to grow, the QM rubric will continue to be revised, to take into account new developments and new information on student success. Future iterations of the rubric will enable me to keep my courses up-to-date with the literature on student success. My institution requires that all online courses meet QM expectations. By using the rubric, the department is better able to ensure that courses with multiple sections are comparable. Not every instructor uses exactly the same activities but each instructor has to show how those activities align with our common course objectives. Students are learning the same things; they are just learning them in different ways. Using the rubric, especially the standards related to alignment of objectives and assessments/activities, has made it easier to extract data for our department review and course assessment process. We are able to demonstrate precisely how each objective is being achieved. I think the next big use for the rubric is to assess face-to-face classes. The rubric's focus on accessibility, alignment and transparency to students is relevant to synchronous, in-person classes as well. The rubric really is a guide for good teaching. In my department, we have already taken some standards and asked all faculty to use them in their syllabi and teaching. How can you use QM in your own course? Many institutions and state consortiums belong to QM. If they subscribe, you have access to the full rubric and can request a course review from the institutional representative at your school. If your institution does not subscribe, you can ask the eLearning or Distance Learning office to become a part of Quality Matters. If that is not an option, you can still look at the rubric at http://www.qmprogram.org/rubric and use it to help improve your own course. You can incorporate many of QM's principles even without an official review. You can also take QM courses at non-subscriber prices and learn to improve your course by applying some of the rubric to its design. In closing, I would recommend Quality Matters as a way to improve online (and hybrid as well as face-to-face) classes by focusing on design issues, thereby freeing the instructor to focus on content and on interaction with students. Ultimately increased student success and satisfaction can result.

References

Allen, I. E., & Seaman, J. (November 2011). Going the distance: Online education in the United States, 2011. Retrieved from: http://www.onlinelearningsurvey.com /reports/goingthedistance.pdf

Instructional Technology Council. (March, 2012). 2011 Distance education survey results: Trends in eLearning: Tracking The impact of eLearning at community colleges. Retrieved from: http://www.itcnetwork.org/attachments /article/87/ITCAnnualSurveyMarch2012.pdf

Ke, F., & Xie, K. (2009). Toward deep learning in adult-oriented online courses: The impact of course design strategies. *The Internet and Higher Education, 12*(3–4), 136–145. http://dx.doi.org/10.1016/j.iheduc.2009 .08.001

Quality Matters. (2012) Underlying Principles of Quality Matters. Retrieved from: http://www.qmprogram.org

Swan, K., Matthews, D., Bogle, L., Boles, E., & Day, S. (2011). Linking online course design and implementation to learning outcomes: A design experiment. *The Internet and Higher Education.* doi:10.1016/j.iheduc.2011.07.002

MANAGING THE CLASSROOM

It was one of those conversations that deans hope to avoid. A student asks for an appointment and you discover during the meeting the student's agenda is to complain about a course. In this case, the professor and the syllabus had promised ten unannounced short quizzes over reading assignments spread throughout the semester which, when combined, would account for ten percent of the final course grade.

However, the professor had only gotten around to offering three of these quizzes, so now each quiz would be weighted much more heavily in the computation of the final course grade than the syllabus and the professor had indicated. The student had a point, the professor's lack of organization and planning had changed the calculation of the course grade, making what appeared to be low-stakes quizzes into higher-stakes assessments after the quizzes had been completed. While I steered the student back to the professor and then potentially to the department chair to address his concerns rather than coming directly to the dean, it was clear to me that the student had a legitimate objection. The faculty member involved failed to provide the promised structure and opportunities which were described in the course syllabus. It was not an instructor decision made with forethought; it was the outcome of a lack of classroom organization and planning.

In my view, classroom organization and management are greatly underappreciated and often overlooked aspects of effective teaching. When a professor fails to provide structure to a class or fails to make that structure apparent to students, students spend their time and energy trying to decipher where the class is headed during a given session instead of being focused on learning. Sometimes the structure of the class session is clear in our own minds, but we fail to make it apparent to students. This lack of clarity can easily undermine student learning.

It is easy to see how a lecture needs structure. It's always a good idea to provide a brief outline of the material to be discussed in a lecture, to make clear the organization of the presentation of the material through numbering or bullet points, and to recap frequently ("We've said three things in response to this question..."). Providing such structure helps students to see material as more than a bunch of disconnected information. It allows students to understand how an argument is made and how evidence and logic are brought to bear. Seeing how the pieces fit together enables students to understand the bigger picture, perceive relationships, and develop higher-order thinking skills.

However, it is not merely lectures which require classroom structure and management. All aspects of classroom pedagogy need careful forethought, planning, structure, and management. Effective discussions are rarely spontaneous. Discussions that delve into the heart of the issue are much more likely to occur when a faculty member has structured the conversation by carefully planning questions to steer students toward important issues and critical reflection. They happen when an instructor intentionally builds them into the class session rather than simply hoping that a productive discussion will spontaneously "erupt" during class.

The contributors to this chapter on classroom management provide us with valuable guidance and strategies which can facilitate more effective teaching and greater student learning. Carrier, Mitchell, and Sloane present both what they call prevention strategies—designed to clarify expectations and build rapport with students and reactive strategies—for dealing with issues which occasionally arise in class. Both designing a course to make expectations clear and anticipating potential problems and how to deal with them make for more effective classroom management. Miles Free, who teaches in an MBA program, describes the strategies he utilizes to empower students and transform them from "compliant worker bees" to "critical thinkers" by creating ground rules for "safe" discussion and engaging students emotionally with the material.

Most faculty members recognize the benefits that come from student engagement in meaningful class discussions, but determining how to motivate and assess participation is a challenge. Tony Docan-Morgan provides a system for assessing student participation in classroom discussion that requires students to reflect upon their contributions. Recognizing that many adjuncts do not have office space which would allow them to be personally assessable to students, Elizabeth Connell describes her use of a virtual learning environment, such as Blackboard, to organize course materials and make them readily available to students.

The next two selections focus on another aspect of the classroom that we often assume and hope will arise spontaneously, but is much more successfully achieved when carefully planned and structured—community building. Shane Brady describes how to utilize a critical pedagogy approach to build community through a step by step "developing community values" activity. Zach Thieneman offers some simple, yet effective techniques for developing community in online courses.

Elena Doludenko provides guidance on how to balance student participation in class with a technique developed for a foreign language course that is applicable in course of all types. Mark Bradford, recognizing that sometimes students need motivation to both attend class and be prepared for class, describes how he utilizes Expectancy Theory to motivate attendance and preparation. Addressing the challenge of keeping students engaged in class, Jess Gregory presents a peer-to-peer feedback strategy. Finally, Kevin Krahenbuhl wraps up the chapter with lessons learned from the attempt to move from lecture to cooperative learning strategies. Krahenbuhl's insights remind us that a critical element of good teaching is careful classroom management that involves forethought, planning, and structure—traits exhibited in each quick hit in this chapter.

JAY HOWARD
BUTLER UNIVERSITY

MANAGING PROBLEMATIC CLASSROOM SITUATIONS

JONATHAN CARRIER
LARAMIE COUNTY COMMUNITY COLLEGE

Jonathan Carrier is the department chair of Math and Sciences at the Albany County Campus of Laramie County Community College and has been a psychology instructor for the past eight years. As part of this position, Jonathan supervises numerous adjunct faculty in History, Sociology, Psychology, Mathematics, and a variety of science courses.

NATHANAEL G. MITCHELL
SPALDING UNIVERSITY

Nathanael G. Mitchell is an assistant professor in the School of Professional Psychology at Spalding University. He was an adjunct professor himself for three years early in his career and is now in a training role mentoring new faculty and lecturers.

NORAH C. SLONE
SPALDING UNIVERSITY

Norah C. Slone is an assistant professor in the School of Professional Psychology at Spalding University. She has been a lecturer for the past year and received invaluable mentorship from a co-author on the paper.

Keywords: Classroom Management, Student Behavior

Framework

A well-managed class, regardless of the subject matter, can mean the difference between an enjoyable, academically successful semester and a long, tedious one for both students and instructors. Instructors who are proactive in planning for specific issues are likely to be more successful than those who are reactive in only dealing with problematic situations after they have occurred. Well-managed classrooms may be achieved through a thoughtful approach that blends both prevention strategies as well as those that are reactive.

Making it Work

Prevention. Two primary prevention strategies that may be useful to include are clarifying expectations and establishing rapport with students. First, a major source of student dissatisfaction and conflict is the perception that an instructor's expectations are unclear, unfair, unstable, or nonexistent (CFE, 2004). Therefore, having clear and well-crafted syllabi and rubrics that detail expectations, assignments, and due dates may assuage student anxiety and quash problems before they begin (Afros & Schryer, 2009).

Second, establishing rapport with students can create a positive learning environment. Students who believe their instructors care about them are more positively disposed toward the course and the instructor (Feldman, 1989).

Rapport can be established by sharing appropriate information about themselves, learning students' names and small details about their lives, responding quickly to e-mails and phone calls, and encouraging respectful questioning throughout the course.

Reactive strategies. Although prevention will head off many potential student issues, problems will invariably arise from time to time. The effective management of these problems during, before, and after class sessions can help keep minor issues from becoming more concerning. The following circumstances are non-emergency situations that are common in many classrooms across fields of study.

It is not uncommon for students to disrespect or attempt to engage instructors or another student in a battle of wills. It is important to gently clarify what the student meant by the disruption before deciding in what way to respond to the comment. In situations where the student has truly "stepped over the line," a private conversation with the student may be necessary. When disrespect is clear, an instructor may need to address the situation immediately and directly in class to model setting appropriate boundaries.

Other class session disruptions can take many shapes and forms, but commonly involve students leaving frequently, too early, arriving late, and/or distraction with food or cell phones/technology. Guidelines for such disruptions should be previously addressed in the instructor's syllabus, but it is generally a good idea to remind the student privately, at least once, about these issues before implementing any penalty. As always, communicate with the student to clarify any misperceptions, ensure there is not an acceptable reason for these issues (e.g., medical concern, sick child; Amada, 1999; Rodriguez, 2008) and remain faithful to your policy if deemed appropriate.

Some students can be overtly disinterested or disengaged in the course as evidenced by appearing "checked out" or asleep during class. If one or two students are clearly bored or otherwise disinterested, instructors should try to find ways to involve them. If many students in the class seem "checked out," the instructor might consider changing their approach to involve students more or have students work in groups (Brophy, 2006). If the same students routinely fall asleep, such behavior may warrant a private conversation to understand why they are sleeping, as there may be medical, mental health, or "life" issue responsible (Amada, 1999). Such conversations may allow you to suggest ways for students to stay awake (i.e., stand at the back of the class, sit at the front) in order to increase their engagement in class.

Students may also attempt to dominate class discussions. They may have a high interest or a great deal of knowledge in the subject matter, be an excited first-time or returning student, or even crave the limelight. Handling such issue may need to be delicate, as instructors do not want to "turn off" an engaged and excited student. Actively calling on other students that are making eye contact with the instructor and seem interested in engaging in the discussion can encourage others to "jump in." It can also be effective to privately thank the student for their enthusiasm, but also encourage them to invite his/her peers to speak up in the class (Amada, 1999).

Some students are unaware of (or do not care about) appropriate social boundaries and may make sexual references, flirt, or say other inappropriate things. In rare cases, students may even do inappropriate things. Although uncomfortable, instructors should intervene firmly and swiftly (Rodriguez,

2008). If the instructor feels safe in doing so, she or he can have a private conference with the student to debrief the situation. If a student is repeatedly and/or grossly inappropriate, a referral should be made to the dean, counseling center, and possibly campus security. It is imperative, that adjuncts be familiar with University policy/guidelines regarding student misconduct. Adjunct professors must act in accordance with such policies to ensure that egregious student behavior is managed properly.

Future Implications

Problems inevitably arise in life and in the classroom; being well informed about strategies to effectively manage problems leads to decreased anxiety and professional confidence. Students and instructors will benefit from the implementation of preventative and reactive strategies to promote effective classroom management. Strategies mentioned above may assist adjunct faculty in creating an environment that is conducive to student learning and maximizes enjoyment for both students and instructors.

References

Afros, E., & Schryer, C. F. (2009). The genre of syllabus in higher education. *Journal of English for Academic Purposes, 8*, 224–233. doi: 10.1016/j.jeap.2009.01.004

Amada, G., & Smith, M. C. (1999). *Coping with misconduct in the college class-room: A practical model.* Asheville, NC: College Administration Publications.

Brophy, J. (2006). History of research on classroom management. In C. M. Evertson & C. S. Weinstein (Eds.), *Handbook of classroom management: Research, practice, and contemporary issues* (pp. 17–43). Mahwah, NJ: Lawrence Erlbaum Associates.

Center for Faculty Excellence. (2004). *Managing classroom conflict.* Chapel Hill, NC: University of North Carolina.

Rodriguez, L. (2008). *Foreign language teaching methods: Classroom management.* Retrieved from: http://www.coerll.utexas.edu/methods/pdf/cm/classroom-rodriguez.pdf.

Some students can be overtly disinterested or disengaged in the course as evidenced by appearing "checked out" or asleep during class.

What Does the Adjunct Bring to the Classroom? Hopefully, Not Just Teaching

Miles Free
Walsh University

Miles has taught a variety of MBA courses since 2008 including Organizational Effectiveness, International Business, Organizational Systems and Design, and Social Media Marketing as an adjunct at Walsh University. He was the lead developer of the Walsh MBA Quality and Performance Management course in 2013, which he has taught in class and online.

Keywords: Chatham House Rules, Thayer Method, Perry Scheme of Intellectual and Ethical Development, Emotional Challenge, Learning Laboratory, Flipped Classroom, Thievery Corporation

Teaching graduate students in an MBA curriculum presents different challenges than traditional teaching in an undergraduate program. In the undergraduate program, teaching drives learning of material, yet the teacher is responsible for material being learned. Graduate education is about domain mastery—holding the student responsible for learning.

The object of my practice is to empower my students with new "Tools They Can Use" and to change their behavior from that of compliant "Worker Bee" to one of "Critical Thinker." This quick hit will describe some of the classroom tools, techniques and performances that I use to foster student learning and critical thinking by creating an emotionally challenging "learning laboratory," rather than a traditional lecture model. The techniques that this approach utilizes include the Chatham House Rule, Thayer Method, Perry Schema, and emotionally challenging "Flipped Classroom" resources peripheral to the main topic. These "Flipped Resources" provide an unexpected emotional connection to the material to challenge the students' secure, prior held beliefs, creating opportunity for exploring alternatives and personal growth.

The Chatham House Rule is the foundation of all classroom discussion. It provides a basis for safe discussion about relevant and actual issues that each student may have. "When a meeting, or part thereof, is held under the Chatham House Rule, participants are free to use the information received, but neither the identity nor the affiliation of the speaker(s), nor that of any other participant, may be revealed." All students agree to hold classroom discussions under the Chatham House Rule, and create a mutual trust that the issues that they bring and share from others will not be taken outside the classroom. We have not had any breach of this since I started teaching in 2008. Graduate students have experiences that will enrich the discussions of classroom materials. Creating a safe space for such discussions is the responsibility of the adjunct. Chatham House Rule provides

the means to do so. http://www.chathamhouse.org/about/chatham-house-rule

I learned about the Thayer Method while visiting my daughter who is attending United States Military Academy at West Point. In order to maximize the effective use of our time together I structure my classroom time in accordance with the Thayer Method, http://dl.acm.org/citation.cfm?id=584623.

In the Thayer method, the students are required to prepare the material ahead of class, and then the instructor uses the time to probe and exercise the students' mastery of the material. My process involves a "quick quiz" at the start of each class session, to ensure and enforce student compliance. The quick quiz—ten questions and twenty minutes—is given at the beginning of the class. The subsequent review of the quiz answers becomes the assurance that the lecture materials have been covered and understood by the students. Leading the discussion of the answers permits the adjunct faculty to provide additional context, expand the scope of the material, and provide personal experience related to the use of the concepts or tools covered.

The Perry Scheme is the basis for my use of emotional techniques to challenge student's assumptions. Prior to graduate school, compliance and acceptance of authority is an expectation of university teaching. In the graduate classroom, we need critical thinking and students that can challenge the underlying assumptions. The goals that I have for my students are

- They recognize their initial level of knowledge and belief;
- They come to terms with the fact that what they know may not in fact reflect the full reality which they face;
- They learn that there are various ways to better understand and incorporate the new materials and ideas into their existing world view;

■ They have the courage (or is it confidence?) to challenge the assumptions that underlie the problems presented to them by using the tools we have provided.

These bullets are an oversimplification and abridgement of William Perry's Scheme of Intellectual and Ethical Development. http://www.cse.buffalo.edu/~rapaport/perry.positions.html

Emotional Challenges and Classroom as Learning Laboratory

As a newly minted foreman in the steel mills, one of my training experiences involved Morris Massey's classic film, "What You Are Is Where You Were, When" http://www.enterprisemedia.com/product/00122/what-you-are-is-where-you-were-when/

This film was one of the first to explain in behavioral terms the differences between the generational cohorts in the workplace, and why certain motivators or punishments were or were not effective, based on a worker's generational demographic. The main lesson that I learned from this was that the only way to assuredly change behavior in adults was to create a significant emotional event.

I have learned from my teaching that the only way to move students along the Perry Scheme is by creating significant emotional events artificially in the classroom. This helps them move from Perry's "Basic Dualism" position—(there are right/wrong answers, engraved on Golden Tablets in the sky, and the student's task is to learn the Right Solutions)—to one of "Multiplicity" (there are 2 kinds of problems: those whose solutions we know and those whose solutions we don't know yet; Student's task is to learn how to find the Right Solutions); or hopefully "Constructed Knowledge/Commitment" (integration of knowledge learned from others with personal experience and reflection). My goal is to create critical thinkers that can recognize the assumptions and have the courage and ability to challenge them in the proper context. Only by challenging students emotionally can you facilitate this move.

Imagine you are a graduate student in the MBA program at a leading Midwestern U.S. Catholic private business school. You had a great GMAT score, you have relevant finance or accounting or management experience. And your first classroom experience is to discuss why the professor is playing these two YouTube videos by Thievery Corporation: Numbers Game: http://www.youtube.com/watch?v=2xAJVri2a1U; Vampires: http://www.youtube.com/watch?v=jquscqfs-XE.

"Flipping the classroom" to create cognitive dissonance by using relevant but totally unexpected, out-of-context materials leads to questioning, reflection, and emotional challenge of assumptions. Prior to the videos, the consensus in the room was that MBA "Quant work" is in fact good, desirable, and ethical. After the videos, reflection and critical thinking about MBA Quant Work are a result of the dissonance of the content of the videos.

References

Chatham House Rule (Chatham House). Retrieved from: http://www.chathamhouse.org/about/chatham-house-rule

Massey, M. (1986). What you are is where you were, when. Retrieved from: http://www.enterprisemedia.com/product/00122/what-you-are-is-where-you-were-when/

Rapaport, W. J. (2013). William Perry's scheme of intellectual and ethical development. Retrieved from: http://www.cse.buffalo.edu/~rapaport/perry.positions.html

Shell, A. E. (2002). The Thayer method of instruction at the United States Military Academy: A modest history and a modern personal account. *PRIMUS: Problems, resources, and issues in mathematics undergraduate studies.* 12 (1) 27–38.

Thievery Corporation (2008). The numbers game. Retrieved from: http://www.youtube.com/watch?v=2xAJVri2a1U

Thievery Corporation (2009). Vampires. Retrieved from: http://www.youtube.com/watch?v=jquscqfs-XE

"Flipping the classroom" to create cognitive dissonance by using relevant but totally unexpected, out of context materials leads to questioning, reflection, and emotional challenge of assumptions.

THE PARTICIPATION LOG: ASSESSING STUDENTS' CLASSROOM PARTICIPATION

TONY DOCAN-MORGAN
UNIVERSITY OF WISCONSIN, LACROSSE

Dr. Docan-Morgan, a former adjunct instructor, is currently a faculty member in the Department of Communication Studies at University of Wisconsin, La Crosse. In addition to teaching four courses a semester, he is the coordinator of the department's basic communication course, where he works with approximately five faculty members and fifteen lecturers each semester.

Keywords: Classroom Participation, Assessment

Framework

Like many instructors in higher education, I expect my students to participate actively in the classroom—namely to contribute meaningfully to discussion questions posed to the entire class and to work through applied problems and activities in small groups. The benefits of classroom participation are clear: "students who actively participate in the learning process learn more than those who do not" (Weaver & Qi, 2005, p. 570). Further, many college instructors perceive student classroom participation as a factor in learning (Carini, Kuh, & Klien, 2006) and assign students participation grades (Bean & Peterson, 1998; Rogers, 2013). However, classroom participation is difficult to assess, in part because it is difficult to track in a reliable manner (Armstrong & Boud, 1983; Rogers, 2013). My own experiences as a former adjunct and current faculty member mirror many of these findings.

The benefits of classroom participation are clear: "students who actively participate in the learning process learn more than those who do not."

During my first ten years of college teaching, I advocated for my students to participate regularly in class, delineated specific expectations for classroom participation in course syllabi, and recorded the quality and quantity of students' participation after each class session. However, I came to realize the difficulty of assessing students' participation while they worked in small groups. Although I could listen in on groups' conversations, it was simply impossible to observe and assess the quality of each student's contribution to the group. Further, I began teaching larger class sizes, making it unmanageable to assess each student's classroom participation. In response, I developed a "participation log" which students use to record their participation, reflect on improving their participation, and demonstrate that they are participating meaningfully in class. In short, the log allows students to record, self-assess, and work toward improving their participation in class, and aids me in assessing student participation, how students are processing course material, and how I can improve my teaching.

Making it Work

On the first day of class, we discuss participation expectations outlined in the syllabus. Some of these expectations, include:

- Making a substantive, oral contribution during class lecture or large-class discussion at least once a week (e.g., answering questions posed by the instructor, bringing up related and relevant information, linking classroom discussions to assigned readings).
- Staying on task in dyads, small groups, and activities. When given a task or question to discuss, work to make meaningful and course content-driven contributions, ask group-mates questions, and brainstorm additional ideas. Do not shortchange discussions or activities by finishing early.

I also inform students that they will keep a log of their participation. We discuss the log's purpose for the student—to demonstrate an accurate record of the quality and quantity of participation, and to assess and work toward improving one's classroom participation. I also highlight the utility of the log from my perspective—it allows me to assess student participation and understanding of course material, as well as how I can improve instruction. I provide students with a template of the log as a Word document and recommend that students update their logs once or twice a week. The log includes the following information:

1. Participation during lecture or large class discussion. Note that this type of participation refers to making comments heard by the entire class. Students should log approximately 10 specific examples and ensure that they are spread out over the course of the semester.

Date	What did you contribute to lecture or large class discussion? Report what you shared specifically and your perception of how, if at all, your contribution aided the flow of the lecture or discussion, as well as the comment's relevance to the lecture or large class discussion.

2. Participation in dyads, small groups, and activities: Log at least 10 specific examples and ensure that they are spread out over the course of the semester.

Date	What did you contribute to the dyad, small group, and/or activity? Summarize how you participated, and your perception of how, if at all, your participation aided the interaction.

3. Self-assessment, reflection, and improvement: Log two self-assessments of your performance as a participator in the class, focusing on your strengths and how you can improve. Reflect on participation expectations outlined in the syllabus, as well as the quality and quantity of your participation in class. The first self-assessment should be completed between weeks 3–7, and the second should be completed between weeks 8–12. Each self-assessment should be at least 5 sentences in length.

Date	Reflection

I require students to submit their logs at mid-semester and at the end of the semester. Both submissions are graded. The logs are useful for gauging the quality and quantity of each student's participation and their perception of how their participation aids classroom discussions. I find that many students' self-assessments at mid-semester focus on how they need to improve (i.e., "I need to participate more frequently and consistently"; "I should link discussion responses directly to class readings"), and often need little elaboration from me.

I provide individual, written feedback to students, which frequently corroborates their self-assessment and/or offers additional recommendations for successful participation (i.e., "since your group sometimes finishes the activity and discussion early, work to ask group members to elaborate on their points"; "push the discussion by considering solutions that have not been considered"). I am rarely confronted with a "fudged" participation log, in part because I remind students that I also monitor and record their contributions.

Future Implications

As a result of reviewing hundreds of students' participation logs for the past two years, I am more aware of their experiences as active (and sometimes inactive) classroom participators, and as a result have improved my teaching practice. The mid-semester and end-of-semester logs provide useful, albeit indirect data regarding student learning. Some students, for example, articulate confusion about course concepts in their logs. I am able to revisit and clarify course material at mid-semester and revise classroom discussion questions and activities for the future. Reading and reflecting on students' self-assessments has also improved my skill as a facilitator of classroom discussions and activities. I am more sensitive to and aware of students' voices in my classes, and better equipped to respond to and synthesize student contributions.

References

Armstrong, M., & Boud, D. (1983). Assessing participation in discussion: An assessment of the issues. *Studies in Higher Education, 8*(1), 33–44.

Bean, J. C., & Peterson, D. (1998). Grading classroom participation. *New Directions for Teaching and Learning, 74,* 33–40.

Carini, R. M., Kuh, G. D., &. Klien, S. P. (2006). Student engagement and student learning: Testing the linkages. *Research in Higher Education, 47*(1), 1–32.

Rogers, S. L. (2013). Calling the question: Do college instructors actually grade participation? *College Teaching, 61,* 11–22.

Weaver, R. R., & Qi, J. (2005). Classroom organization and participation: College students' perceptions. *The Journal of Higher Education, 76*(5), 570–601.

Keep It Central

Elizabeth B. Connell
Richard Stockton College of New Jersey

After 20 years of working as a bench chemist, technical writer, software trainer, and business owner, I transitioned to teaching as an adjunct at The Richard Stockton College of New Jersey. For the past two years, I have taught a face-to-face class, Writing and Editing for the Health Sciences, for the School of Health Sciences.

Keywords: Virtual Learning Environment, Academic Honesty, Online Marking

Most adjuncts work remotely and do not have on-campus office locations accessible to students. To improve student-adjunct communication, adjunct instructors must centralize course materials and communication channels. A virtual learning environment (VLE), such as Blackboard, provides adjuncts with a one-stop-shop for organizing any college classroom — online, hybrid, or face to face. Blackboard provides the adjunct with a single repository for housing course materials; creating assignments and tests; monitoring academic honesty; electronically marking papers; publishing a gradebook; and communicating with students via email, blogging, and wikis.

Centralizing course materials reduces student confusion about course requirements and due dates. The adjunct instructor can publish contact information, syllabi, course documents, videos, web links, and presentations in Blackboard. When publishing course documents, instructors should consider using a chronological organizational method. It mimics the syllabus format and is easy for students to follow. If a student misses class, the missed coursework is already available in Blackboard. When teaching class, the instructor should use the Blackboard class page to familiarize students with the layout and accessibility of information.

Integrating tests inside Blackboard allows students to get feedback and see grades more quickly. Test questions can be multiple choice, short answer, or essay. For future tests, the instructor can reuse or rework questions. The instructor can program Blackboard to calculate and upload the grade to the gradebook automatically, or the instructor can review each question before the final grade is calculated. To ensure academic honesty during the testing process, the instructor can password protect access to the test, limit student time on the test, and use a program such as LANSchool to prevent application or Web use.

To monitor academic honesty, the adjunct can use the Blackboard Turnitin plugin to create writing assignments. When the assignment is due, the student uploads the assignment to Turnitin Blackboard. Turnitin automatically creates an Originality Report and Similarity Index for the instructor and student to review. Turnitin highlights and numerically marks any indications of plagiarism. Instructors have the option of using the Originality report as a teaching tool by allowing multiple uploads; thus, allowing students to fix errors before the due date.

A survey of students found the majority of students could decipher the online comments more easily.

• • • • • • • • • • • •

In addition to plagiarism detection, Blackboard Turnitin GradeMark provides paper marking functionality. The instructor can use Turnitin GradeMark to mark student papers electronically using colored bubble comments, typed suggestions, and voice recordings. The instructor can set a date that these comments and grades are available to students. If an instructor requires revisions on a paper, he or she can create a new assignment called Revision 1, Revision 2, etc. Any time during the semester, the instructor can click on the student's name and review all student papers, comments, grades, and student time spent revising. At the end of the semester, the student can move his or her portfolio of work into the Content section of Blackboard, to create a professional, portable, HTML style portfolio.

Usually, Blackboard automatically connects to each student's university email account. Via Blackboard, the instructor can send emails to the whole class, groups, or individuals. In the Blackboard Groups section, the instructor can assign students to multiple groups. Within the group, members can communicate via email, blogs, wikis, and file exchange. To monitor group communication, the instructor should add his or her name to each group. This is extremely useful for keeping group projects on track, monitoring student interactions, and making sure that all students in the group participate.

Most universities offer free courses on Blackboard or other VLE functionality. Last semester, I conducted a case study to compare the use of handwritten paper marking versus online paper marking via Blackboard Turnitin GradeMark. A survey of students found the majority of students could decipher the online comments more easily, and they spent more time reviewing and revising their work. Most importantly, the study revealed that students who missed class stayed on task because their marked papers were available online instead of in the instructor's briefcase.

FLIPPING THE CLASSROOM

ROBIN K. MORGAN
INDIANA UNIVERSITY SOUTHEAST

Robin is currently a professor of psychology and serves as the university director of the Faculty Colloquium on Excellence in Teaching. As a graduate student, she also taught as an adjunct faculty member at a community college.

Keywords: Flipping, Teaching Technique

Okay, so you've heard the term. You've even considered the idea of flipping your classroom. And, yet, you hesitate to commit as it sounds like a tremendous amount of work.

In a flipped classroom, work is assigned outside of class—typically taking advantage of online videos, quizzes, and presentations—to allow more active learning to occur during class time. Ideally, the flipped classroom approach allows for the most efficacious use of class time. However, without a careful design, the flipped classroom can degenerate into chaos with students arriving to class unprepared and class time being squandered.

How can you successfully flip your class? The following suggestions should prepare you:

- **Share the logic of what you're doing with your students**: Students enter class with pre-set expectations. Attempting to flip a classroom without sharing your expectations and rationale with students may result in student evaluations where students complain that the professor "didn't teach."

- **Assess students' understanding of pre-class assignments:** It's nice to think that students will come prepared to class—and some will. The reality is that students are busy people and are likely to devote their time to completing tasks that are graded. By assessing students' understanding of pre-class assignments—I use simple quizzes or discussion questions—the number of students who complete the pre-class assignments increases dramatically. This is critical to ensure my in-class activities are successful. This also allows me to see what students understand before they come to class. I can then adjust what is covered in class to address material not well understood.

- **Align pre-class assignments with class activities:** The stronger the connection is between pre-class assignments and class activities, the easier it is for students to understand the importance of the pre-class activities and to believe that the activities in class are important. If students come to believe that in-class activities are not important, they will frequently stop coming to class.

- **Assessments must reflect both pre-class assignments and in-class activities:** Building assessments that complement the flipped model may be more

difficult. This is important as students will quickly figure out if assessment focuses more on pre-class activities or in-class activities.

- **Create engaging materials for outside of class:** Given the ease of lecture capture technology, it is tempting to simply record lectures for students to review outside of class. There is some evidence that students are less likely to continue watching such lectures that last longer than 10–15 minutes. Instead, create minilecture on particularly difficult concepts, use YouTube videos when appropriate, or even incorporate segments from movies or television shows. An assortment of videos, narrated PowerPoints, and readings (from a variety of sources) may be much more effective than a lengthy, recorded lecture.

- **One step at a time:** It isn't necessary to flip your entire class the first time you attempt this approach. Instead, select one or two class sessions that a flipped approach makes sense for your course. Develop the materials and activities for just those one or two class sessions. As you develop more materials and become more comfortable flipping, you can work your work toward an entire flipped course.

BUILDING COMMUNITY IN THE CLASSROOM THROUGH UTILIZING CRITICAL PEDAGOGY

SHANE R. BRADY
UNIVERSITY OF OKLAHOMA

Dr. Brady has been an adjunct professor in social work for the past five years at several institutions. Dr. Brady also developed and created mentorship programs, trainings, and curriculum geared towards supporting the teaching of adjuncts and lecturers. Dr. Brady is now an assistant professor of Social Work at the University of Oklahoma.

Keywords: Critical Pedagogy, Popular Education, Classroom Community Building

Framework

Paulo Freire (1970) states that "education either functions as an instrument which is used to facilitate integration of the younger generation into the logic of the present system and bring about conformity or it becomes the practice of freedom, the means by which men and women deal critically and creatively with reality and discover how to participate in the transformation of their world (p. 34)." Freire's words highlight the essence of critical pedagogy and the foundation for my teaching pedagogy. Critical pedagogy emphasizes the classroom as a communal learning space, critical

dialogue as an essential tool for individual consciousness, minimization of power differentials between students and instructors, and the embracing of conflict and difference as key elements to adult learning (Adams & Horton, 1975; Boal, 1979; Horton & Freire, 1990; Freire, 1970, 1998; Lange, 2004; Zullo & Pratt, 2009).

The focus of this 'quick hit' is on a 'developing community values' activity that I have regularly utilized to engage and build community with students on the first day of class in order to set a positive tone for community building and learning throughout the semester. Through successfully sharing power with students from day one, community begins to form in the classroom, which leads to more engaged and active classroom learning throughout the semester.

Making It Work

The values activity provides a good illustration of how instructors can make use of critical pedagogy in the classroom. By involving students on the first day in an important classroom task, power is shared with students, while power differentials are minimized. Below the process for implementing the activity is provided, but instructors are encouraged to adapt it accordingly to fit the needs of their classes.

Step One (20 Minutes)
Explain to students that you would like them to work in small groups to come up with a fair process for developing classroom values. Deciding on group formation is up to the comfort of the instructor, but I tend to place students into groups of 4–5 for this exercise. During this step, I have students put the major elements of what they talk about in bullet points on large easel paper.

Step 2 (10 Minutes)
After all groups have transferred the key elements of their fair process to the large easel paper, I prompt everyone to walk around and look at what other groups have come up with and to take note of the similarities and differences between them as well as any critical insights that they may have while reading through them.

Step 3 (30–45 Minutes)
In this step, I encourage smaller groups to talk about with the class what things they saw as important for ensuring a fair process to developing classroom values. Students are also encouraged to discuss their insights and reactions to what other groups bring up and talk about. I also create a space for quieter students to talk by designating a block of time, such as five minutes, where only those who have not yet spoken, can provide their perspectives.

Step 5 (10–15 Minutes)
In order to encourage participation from everyone, I let students know that I will be creating a Google Document so that we can continue this activity over the course of the semester. Through the use of a Google Document, all students can participate anonymously, so even if some students are not comfortable participating in the classroom portion of the activity, they can still participate through the Google Document. I instruct students that they can add values to the Google Document as they see fit, but may not change anything that has been written by other students.

Step 6 (Ongoing)
At the beginning of the second class, I pull up the Google Document and have students look over it. I will often make arrangements to do this portion of the activity in a space with access to computers or provide laptops for those who may not have them. We then discuss the Google Document, values presented in the document by students, and the process of the values activity. I let students know that because of the difference in values among community members as well as the dynamic nature of the classroom community, students are encouraged to continue adding to the Google Document as the semester goes on and we will periodically pull it out and discuss new additions to the document in subsequent classes.

Spending time on engaging students... will pay dividends throughout the semester.

Assessment of Activity
Assessment of the community values activity is important as it has helped me to make small changes to the activity over time based on student feedback. Assessment of this activity is done by way of qualitative student feedback after classes one and two and by way of brief anonymous student comments written onto note cards that I provide to them. Student feedback has been overwhelmingly positive, but constructive feedback has been used to improve the activity over the years.

Future Implications

One of the most difficult aspects of this activity is that it takes time to properly implement. While class time may often be in short supply, spending time on engaging students and including them in building the classroom community will pay dividends throughout the semester. Finally, implementing this activity in the classroom has forced me to learn how to share power with students and be more open to student feedback and critique, which has helped me to grow as an instructor.

References

Adams, F., & Horton, M. (1975). *Unearthing seeds of fire: The idea of highlander*. Winston-Salem, NC: Blair.

Boal, A. (1979). *Theatre of the oppressed*. (C. McBride, & M. O. Leal-McBride, Trans.) New York: Theatre Communications Group.

Freire, P. (1970). *Pedagogy of the oppressed*. NewYork: Continuum International.

Freire, P. (1998). P*edagogy of freedom: Ethics, democracy, and courage*. Lanham, Maryland: Rowman & Littlefield Publishers Inc.

Horton, M., & Freire, P. (1990). We make the road by walking. In B. Bell, J. Gaventa, & J. Peters (Eds.), *Conversations on education and social change* (pp. 227–249). Philadelphia: Temple University Press.

Lange, E. A. (2004). Transformative and restorative learning: A vital dialectic for sustainable societies. *Adult Education Quarterly*, *54*(2), 121–139. doi:10.1177 /0741713603260276

Zullo, R., & Pratt, G. (2009). Critical pedagogy as a tool for labor-community coalition building. *Journal of Community Practice*, *17*(1), 140–156. doi:10.1080 /107054209028.62132

BUILDING RELATIONSHIPS IN ONLINE CLASSES

ZACK THIENEMAN
SPALDING UNIVERSITY

Zack is finishing his doctorate degree in clinical psychology and his dissertation focuses on student and faculty attitudes towards online teaching and learning.

DEDE WOHLFARTH
SPALDING UNIVERSITY

DeDe Wohlfarth is a full-time faculty member at Spalding University who is still semi-clueless in teaching online, despite having made significant gains in doing so.

Keywords: Best Practices, Student Relationships, Online Teaching

Learning is a process which requires interacting with material to promote integration and retention. In face-to-face and online courses, considerable evidence supports the relationship between students to students and students to instructors as integral pieces of learning (Dykman & Davis, 2008; Pelz, 2010; Elias, 2010). However, establishing relationships in an online format can be a daunting task. Here are some tried and true methods to increase student/student and student/instructor relationships that have worked for us:

- Write a welcome e-mail that conveys your excitement about the students and course materials. A welcome e-mail has shown to increase student motivation and attitude (Legg & Wilson, 2009).
- Create an introduction thread with concrete, specific questions. These questions may be professional or personal in nature, such as asking student's career trajectory, hobbies or favorite restaurants. As in face-to-face classes, lead by example. Starting the thread with a model shows students what is expected and provides a template for them. Simple ways to make this more engaging include providing a picture and asking a variety of questions.

- Provide instructor videos of lecturettes relevant to course topics. A short lecture of important material helps students see the personality of the instructor in a new way and increases the student/instructor relationship by allowing the student to physically see the instructor. It is okay if these videos are filmed outside of the classroom, are not professionally edited, and contain "bloopers." The inevitable "blooper" is entertaining and can be used to teach material or to build connection between the students and instructor.
- Give prompt, detailed, and personalized feedback. Feedback is an easy way to develop a relationship with students and is especially important in online classes (Savery, 2010). Feedback given within a pre-specified timeframe which outlines explicit rationale for critique helps promote student learning and develop the student/instructor relationship.
- Have an optional discussion thread that provides links to and discussions about current events connected to your subject. By engaging in these discussions, students identify like-minded peers who help deepen their understanding of course material. Reward participation

with extra credit points and frequent postings of your own, including specific praise for students who post thoughtful comments and add resources.

- Self-disclose more than you would in a face-to-face class since students do not get the visual and informal cues to see "who we are" as instructors in online classes. Be open about mistakes and model learning for students. This includes sharing when you don't know something. These behaviors help build trust in the student/instructor relationship.

- Students can develop relationships with other students through requiring them to review each other's homework assignments. This promotes interaction between students and builds trust while employing critical thinking skills. It also deepens understanding of the subject matter.

- Depending on the size of the class and technological sophistication of the students, have students introduce themselves by video instead of text. A short video (less than one minute) can help them see each other's personality without being a time burden.

These suggestions help build relationships in online classrooms. Like in face-to-face teaching, creativity is paramount in providing students innovative ways to engage with course material, the instructor, and other students!

References

Dykman, C. A., & Davis, C. K. (2008). Online education forum: Part two—teaching online versus teaching conventionally. *Journal of Information Systems Education, 19,* 157–164.

Elias, T. (2010). Universal instructional design principles for Moodle. *International Review of Research in Open and Distance Learning, 11*(2). Retrieved from: http://www.irrodl.org/index.php/irrodl/article/view/869/1575

Legg, A. M., & Wilson, J. H. (2009). E-mail from professor enhances student motivation and attitudes. *Teaching of Psychology, 36*(3), 205–211. doi:10.1080/00986280902960034

Pelz, B. (2010). (My) Three principles of effective online pedagogy. *Journal of Asynchronous Learning Networks, 14*(1), 103–116.

Savery, J. R. (2010). BE VOCAL: Characteristics of successful online instructors. *Journal of Interactive Online Learning, 9*(3), 141–152.

ONE CLASS, TWELVE STUDENTS, FIVE STATIONS

ELENA DOLUDENKO
INDIANA UNIVERSITY

Elena Doludenko has taught Russian as an associate instructor for the past 3 years at IU.

Keywords: Engaging Students, Review of Material, Creating Positive Attitude

One of the challenges of teaching a foreign language at a college level is that you need to manage the class period in a way that gives every student a chance to speak and, at the same time, keeps other students occupied. It becomes a challenge with up to 20 students in a class. At the same time, students get tired of the routine exercises and drills (as the class usually meets 4–5 times a week), so an instructor has to be creative while choosing the activities.

I developed a series of short games/activities to review the future tense for second-year Russian. The activities were distributed in-class, and students had to change activity stations every 8 minutes. They worked in pairs or groups of 4 depending on the game. The first two stations included cards with the different role-play situations that students needed to act out (e.g., "One of you invites the other for Thanksgiving. Ask about what you will be doing together."). The next two stations had a stack of cards with pictures, and students worked in pairs, taking turns being the "fortune-teller." The fortune teller would take a card and make up a sentence with the image on it in the future tense, thus "predicting" the future. Four students played "Go Fish!" at the fourth station where, instead of pictures, they needed to match the sentences in the future tense by asking questions (e.g., a student asks, "Bob, will you be doing homework all weekend?" If Bob has a card with the same sentence, he says, "Yes, I will be doing homework all weekend" and passes the card to the student. If he does not have the card, he says, "No, I won't be doing homework all weekend. Go fish!"). Thus, during the class, all students were engaged, had an opportunity to speak, and reviewed the material. They also enjoyed playing and making up "predictions" for each other, thus leaving the classroom with positive emotions. Students said that such informal activities help them to remember material better and made them less conscious of the fact that they were speaking a foreign language.

These activities helped students to work at their own pace, and they could ask me individual questions any time while I walked from station to station, which turned out to be another benefit of these activities. Having different stations also allowed students to move around the classroom and change activities every few minutes, which helped with the class appear to go faster. As a modification, the same format could be held in a computer lab where students (in pairs or groups) complete different assignments on a computer to learn, produce, or review the material. Even though this activity is specific to a language class, the idea of different stations for reviewing in pairs or groups can be used for other disciplines as well as a tool for keeping students' attention focused on the material at hand.

Using Expectancy Theory and Small Win Theory for Classroom Success

Mark Bradford
Indiana University at South Bend

Mark has been an associate instructor in the Judd Leighton School of Business and Economics for 10 years. He has been awarded merit status as well as being named Associate Professor of the Year in 2012.

Keywords: Expectancy Theory, Motivating Students, Small Wins, Classroom Management

Framework

Many instructors have trouble motivating students to regularly attend class, let alone keeping them engaged in class through the semester. I was no different. However, after stumbling around for a few years, I discovered a fairly simple way of making sure students come to class having already read the material AND continue attending class. The added plus is that classes become ones that students "hate to miss." The answer is derived from understanding the concept of Vroom's Expectancy Theory, which says that in order to keep people motivated, there are three main considerations. Simply stated, Vroom's Theory states that people will "do the work if there is a strong expectation that the work will be rewarded AND if the reward is important to the individual."

Fairly simple way of making sure students come to class having already read the material.

In my classroom I discovered that if I rewarded the students with a tangible extrinsic reward (a grade) for coming to class

prepared, the students would not only come to class regularly, but they would also feel better about themselves. That discovery has led to success at both the freshman level and the senior level. It makes teaching class very rewarding for me as well and has created some incredible synergy between the students and myself.

The best news it, it is simple to implement.

Making it Work

The first night of class, I inform the students that there will be a quiz at the beginning of class nearly every day of the semester. Yes, they groan and roll their eyes. That is when I introduce the class mission statement, which is as follows:
To get an A in this class you must:
1. Show Up On Time.
2. Be Prepared.
3. Be Enthusiastic.

Then I tell them that they will be expected to read the relevant chapter BEFORE coming to class and they will be given a 10-point OPEN-NOTE quiz on the material. The quiz will start exactly at the beginning of class.

For example, if the class is scheduled to start at 1 PM, the quiz goes on the overhead screen exactly at 1 PM and is pulled off exactly at 1:10 PM. If a student shows up at 1:05, they have five minutes to complete the quiz. If they show up at 1:10 or later, they do not get to take the quiz. Then I go over the quiz immediately so the students get to verify the answers. I allow for three missed quizzes in the overall grade for incidental absences but if they take all 16 quizzes, they, in effect, get those three scores as bonus.

Obviously, several students beg and plead with me to allow them to take their missed quizzes, but I make this a zero-exception policy. They get to use their notes on exams as well, but the exams tend to be less definition and more application which requires them to show that they actually understand the concept (and I go over the concept and application in class). In addition, I rarely lecture the entire class. Instead I break the class into 20-minute "bits of activity." The highly motivated students LOVE it. Go figure.

But I have discovered that the average student also loves it because it puts the responsibility for their grade directly on them. If they take the notes and show up for class on time, they usually get an average of 9+ on the quizzes. This encourages the average student to come to class because they have a chance for the elusive (to them) A grade. In short, I reward hard work and responsibility over rote memorization and lecture. I even call the reward system "getting paid," and it leads to a discussion of extrinsic rewards versus intrinsic rewards. "If you do the work of making notes and showing up on time," I say. "You will get paid by doing well on the quiz by scoring an average of nine points per quiz. It is just like getting paid at work. If you show up on time and do your work, you will get paid real money. My version of pay is by giving you an A." However, there are certain students who do not respond, especially at the freshman level. I do NOT ignore those students, nor do I write them off as losers. Vroom's Expectancy Theory gives me the answer to why they do not do the work. Vroom's would simply say that the reward is not important to that student. Eureka!

I can quit blaming myself for losing these students, but it does not absolve me of my responsibility of trying to get them to succeed. Instead of designating these students offhand as "deadbeats," I will focus in on the ones having trouble about 3–4 weeks into the class. Normally I will discover they are either just not interested in the topic for a myriad of reasons and they are perfectly happy with a C or lower, or they have what I call a "structural problem." Many of my students work full-time, or have financial issues, or undependable transportation, etc ...

Once I discover the actual issue behind the poor performance, I can counsel the student. In some cases where the student is failing more classes than just mine because of these issues, I simply suggest the student drop the class for now and come back when they are better prepared to be successful. In the very rare case where the student's issue exists only in my class, we work on that.

Future Implications

The results? My student approval ratings are very high and I keep getting recognized for excellence in my department. More importantly, I teach the students the value of developing good habits as a way of being successful in real life.

Showing up on time and being prepared and enthusiastic are also valuable habits to employers, it seems.

In conclusion, I have been very successful using Vroom's Theory of Motivation in my classroom. I combine its use with other motivational techniques to create what has proven to be a successful classroom experience.

References

Schmidt, C. T. (N.D.). Motivation: Expectancy theory. Retrieved from: http://www.uri.edu/research/lrc/scholl/webnotes/Motivation_Expectancy.htm

I can quit blaming myself for losing these students, but it does not absolve me of my responsibility of trying to get them to succeed.

Fostering Meaningful Peer Interactions: Going Beyond the Nice

Jess L. Gregory
Southern Connecticut State University

Dr. Gregory started in higher education as an adjunct professor. Now full time, she coordinates two courses in Educational Leadership and Policy Studies and works with adjunct faculty teaching those and other courses, sharing and receiving ideas to improve student outcomes across the program.

Keywords: Feedback, Peer Learning, Student Engagement

Framework

In a leadership preparation course at the graduate level, students are frequently asked to present materials to their peers. At times, the audience members during these presentations appear to tune out, undermining the intent of having near peers teaching. To address this, the assignment was changed to include an evaluation of how well the presenter used adult learning theory to engage the audience at multiple levels, but this was only marginally successful. The presentations were of a slightly higher quality, but the audience was still not consistently engaged.

Making it Work

To boost engagement during presentations, I added a requirement: public feedback posted on the class' discussion board. These posts had no pre-determined length, but they were graded. Since these graduate students may not have had sufficient experience providing constructive criticism, the evaluation of the critiques was initially very generous, but as the semester continued, the requirements for the quality of the feedback were increased.

The first feedback was private. After I made a brief presentation, students were asked to provide me with feedback on a 3 x 5 card. They handed in the card and I provided comments on how much the feedback they offered would help me grow as a professional. Basically, I answered the question, was the feedback useful?

Then it was time to have them offer feedback to each other. In as class where there were two mini presentations the students were required to choose one of the two presentations and offer some feedback to the presenters on the class discussion board. The first set of comments was very nice, very general, and not helpful at all. Several students suggested that a group's presentation would be better if they did not turn the lights off and on. As each discussion board post was evaluated in the grade book feature of the learning management system (LMS), I entered a specific comment or

question about how helpful the student's specific comment was. This was time consuming. I also used the announcement feature on the LMS to send and e-mail about the comments overall:

"I know that we had some great presentations, but it is important that you offer some constructive feedback (more than turning the lights on and off). For every presentation, for every educator, for every leader, there are opportunities to improve. Please use the second set of feedback to offer something to the presenters. I was generous in the first set (regardless if you offered or did not offer meaningful feedback for improvement). From this point on, I will be looking for you to thoughtfully offer a suggestion. I know you care about each other, show it through helping everyone improve. :)"

After the individual and whole-class feedback, the second set of presentations generated better critiques. At this point we were at week 6 of a fifteen-week semester. Again, I provided feedback on each comment to the individual student privately through the LMS grade book and publically through an announcement:

"A note on the feedback from last week ... NICE! Almost everyone gave sound feedback, something that would enhance the presentation if it were done again. There was one that was ESPECIALLY GOOD ... this person provided useful feedback and explicitly explained why in terms of learning. This is the new bar for feedback."

Some students capitalized on the opportunity to make revisions to their work and added additional comments to earlier critiques to add how the suggestion they made would improve the learning outcomes of the audience for the presentations. This was not a requirement, but having students go back and make changes was very satisfying.

For the last sets of presentations, the feedback was very specific and useful. Each comment offered by a student was different from the others that were offered earlier on the discussion board and provided the presenter with valuable feedback. While there were no word goals, the later posts were longer and students reported spending more time reading what their peers had written.

Future Implications

Looking back, while I knew that students did not have sufficient experience providing feedback to peers, I assumed they had sufficient experience giving feedback overall because they were educators already. I am not sure this was a safe assumption. I am confident that every educator can tell you the importance of timely and specific feedback, but I am less confident that they are prepared to actually give it.

In the future I will have an explicit conversation about how to provide useful feedback to peers before they give me the first feedback on the 3 x 5 cards. By doing this, I hope to shorten the learning curve. It took nearly half a semester to move the group from providing complementary or irrelevant feedback to giving actionable critique. I believe this is an acceptable amount of time, but my goal would be to have the elements of strong critique develop in the first third of the semester so that there are more opportunities for those behaviors to be reinforced and become habits.

Developing students' ability to provide meaningful feedback was my primary skill goal in this course. There were content related objectives, but as far as developing the individual learner, increasing engagement through peer-to-peer interactions based on providing feedback was paramount. Nicol (2011) states that generating the feedback for a peer is cognitively more demanding than reflecting on the feedback provided by others. By the end of the semester, students were more engaged in the presentation of their peers, they were interacting more during the presentations and asking great questions of the presenter. This improved the quality of the presentations in addition to increasing the level of critique after the presentation.

While this was a graduate level class, I could see using the same techniques of providing feedback on the feedback and gradually escalating the expectations working at every level of higher education where students have access to a LMS with a discussion board.

Reference

Nicol, D. J. (2011). *Peer evaluation in education review*. Retrieved from: http://www.jisc.ac.uk/media/documents/programmes/elearning/ltig/PEERfinalreport.pdf

||||||||||||||||||||||||||||||||||||||||||||||||||||||||||||||||||||||||||||||||||||||||||||||||||||||||||||||||||||||||||||||||||||||||||||||||||||||||||||

Modifying Constructivism for Coherence

Kevin Scott Krahenbuhl
Middle Tennessee State University

Dr. Krahenbuhl was an adjunct professor of history at Dakota State University for four years and an assistant professor of Social Studies for Dakota State's College of Education before joining Middle Tennessee State University. His teaching experience includes traditional, online, hybrid, nightly, and weekend courses and he especially values critical inquiry in pursuit of truth.

Keywords: Constructivism, Guided Learning, Course Design

Framework

As a new faculty member I was bombarded with comments about the problems associated with the lecture. Overwhelmingly, the comments received instilled me with a sense that cooperative learning and constructivism was the model to follow. However, I quickly found out that unless students are given clear guidance and direction, the class would fall into an aimless pursuit of varied interests that formed no coherent picture for the course I was ostensibly teaching. Indeed, critical thinking and creative problem-solving are not developed casually in the course of an undirected exploration (Glenn, 2003).

Making it Work

In redesigning my courses to achieve the values of constructivist pedagogy while maintaining content coherence and integrity I implemented the following five steps. First, I mapped out the big picture—what were the central concepts/ideas relevant for this course? Second, I developed three-to-four "essential questions" under each central concept/idea. Third, I mapped out the semester so that I left two full weeks untouched. Fourth, I developed a class-appropriate project (mine typically involve student creation of a "minidocumentary/video") that students will have free rein in researching, narrating, and producing, with my role simply being a quality-control agent. Those two weeks left untouched are reserved for student peer meetings, collaboration on themes within chosen projects, and presentations of the project findings. And fifth, and finally, I require all students to relate their project topic to one of the course's "essential questions" in a meaningful way. In this way, the final exam can integrate analytical essay questions built directly off those guiding questions and the student's projects provide a designed connection and review in preparation for it.

In each semester since implementing the following changes the class mastery of content has improved and several themes have emerged from student opinion surveys and overall. In the first few semesters (before implementing this model), students overall average grades on quizzes/exams was 59.4%. Since this model has been adopted that overall course average on quizzes/exams is now at 73.7% and although these are not vast numbers, the difference between those is worthy of note. In student opinion surveys, the three most common categories of comments (as determined through open coding) are those related to (a) coherence, (b) challenge, and (c) interesting. In terms of coherence, students are better able to build knowledge on knowledge and see the connections between projects and focused course objectives. Although coming from those who both enjoy and dislike the rigor of the course, students frequently share comments that demonstrate this model is challenging. And finally, the overall engagement of the class has been improved and our learning experience has become more interesting as wild generalizations are less prevalent as students see the connections more clearly.

Future Implications

I have modified this approach for uses in many different types and fields of courses and have found success. As philosopher Roger Scruton said of constructivism: "Even if it were possible to educate [students] in this way one thing is certain: that each generation would know less the one before." I think Scruton was onto something here; namely that unless the experts (trained professionals, e.g., us!) direct the class, the students direct it and disorganization abounds. This approach provides designed synergy between all facets of the course for a coherent learning experience.

References

Glenn, C. (2003). Fanatical secularism. *Education Next, 3* (1) 61–65.

ENHANCING PROFESSIONAL DEVELOPMENT

Professional development is defined as "the advancement of skills or expertise to succeed in a particular profession, esp. through continued education" (Dictionary.com, nd). In other words, professional development is about learning. While most community colleges and universities have some combination of teaching centers, teaching workshops, teaching conferences, peer review/mentoring processes, and professional development programs, such resources are not always as useful to the adjunct faculty member as one might hope. Adjunct faculty may not be on campus at the time such workshops are offered. They may simply not have the time available to attend programs, given other commitments. Or, the programs may not be relevant to instructors who teach quite well but want to develop particular aspects of their teaching. So, while we would strongly encourage adjunct faculty to take advantage of the resources their institution offers, we recognize that adjunct faculty may need to "develop" in other ways.

Guskey (2002; p. 383) posits the following model of teacher change/development:

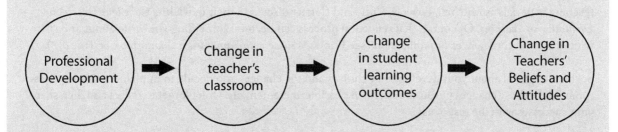

Real change in terms of professional development occurs in a similar manner as our students' learning. We have to do something different. We cannot simply hear about or read about a potential professional development and consider ourselves "developed." We have to try it in the classroom, see if it works to help our students given our disciplinary content and, then, and only then, will we incorporate this new development into our teaching philosophy and repertoire of behaviors. This kind of change holds two disadvantages: 1) it may require significant time and energy and 2) there is always the risk of failure (Guskey, 2002). Given this, we offer the following advice based on our experience with changing our own teaching and with faculty development.: *make changes thoughtfully*, incrementally, and with reflection during and after.

Make changes thoughtfully
There are many sources of potential change in classroom teaching practices. This book is an excellent example of ways to keep your teaching up to date or simply do continual quality improvement. Consider the quick hits in this chapter by Carrier, Mitchell and Slone *Preparing Your Course Before The Semester Begins: Lessons Learned the Hard Way or Developing Effective Syllabi: Key Points for New Instructors* by Mitchell, Fawkes, Slone and Carrier.

We also recommend other Quick Hits volumes as well as more philosophical reads such as *The Courage to Teach* by Parker Palmer or more focused reading such as *Classroom Assessment Techniques* by Angelo and Cross. Of course, there is a wealth of scholarship of teaching and learning in areas such as exploring team based learning, writing practices, student evaluations, using technology and more. Google Scholar is an excellent source for this type of research. Once you read about/discover a potential change, consider: Is this something I could be comfortable doing (most of us have to stretch our comfort zones to make meaningful change)? Is this something that could help my students understand key concepts, skills, or attitudes effectively? Is this something that will work within the time/place constraints of my classroom, virtual or otherwise? Having this conversation with a mentor (see Slone, Mitchell, Carrier and Beauchamp discussion of *Getting Real about Mentorship*) would be an excellent way to thoughtfully consider potential changes.

Make incremental steps
If the answer to the above questions is "yes," then take the leap! You will likely not be convinced this change will work, according to Gusser's (2002) model, until you try it. If possible, make incremental steps—change one unit or one lesson or one class. Do not try to make sweeping changes in everything all at once. If you are incorporating new technology, this is especially true since you may need to learn the technology before you can ask students to use it.

Reflect on the change
Finally, reflect on the change. Any innovation can take a while to work the bugs out. So, do not give up after one try. Gather data about the effects of the change. This could be simply asking students how they felt about the innovation, comparing specific student evaluation items before and after the change (see Embry's quick hit, *Am I a good teacher? What do my evaluations say?*), doing a mid-course evaluation or SGID (see Benton's *Develop Professionally: Listen to Your Students*), looking at particular learning tasks that should reflect the change: writing assignments, test questions etc., or asking a colleague to observe your class or look over teaching materials as Mitchell, Fowkes, Slone and Carrier discuss in their quick hits *Colleague Observation/ Evaluation of Teaching*. Of course, that reflection process can become something you write about and share with others via conferences or publication (see Elrod's *Writing with Familiarity: Comfortable or Trite by?*)

So, be thoughtful about your development choices and the changes you decide to implement in your classroom. Make those changes purposefully and, if possible, incrementally. Don't forget to reflect and then share your successes with the rest of us!

References

Angelo, T. A., & Cross, K. P. (1993). *Classroom assessment techniques: A hand-book for college teachers*. San Francisco: Jossey-Bass.

Guskey, T. R. (2002). Professional development and teacher change. *Teachers and Teaching: Theory and Practice, 8*(3/4), 381–391.

Palmer, P. (1997). *The courage to teach*. San Francisco: Jossey-Bass.

Professional development. (n.d.). Dictionary.com's 21st Century Lexicon. Re-trieved from: http://dictionary .reference.com/browse/professional devel-opment

MARCIA DIXSON
INDIANA-PURDUE FORT WAYNE

JULIE SAAM
IU KOKOMO

DEVELOP PROFESSIONALLY: LISTEN TO YOUR STUDENTS

RAYMOND BENTON, JR.
LOYOLA UNIVERSITY CHICAGO

Raymond Benton, Jr. was, for fourteen years, chair of the department of marketing in the Quinlan School of Business at Loyola University Chicago. As department chair he supervised eleven full-time faculty members and numerous adjunct and part-time instructors.

Keywords: Student Evaluations, Teaching Assessments, Faculty Assessment, Faculty Development, Professional Development

Student course evaluations emerged during the 1960s. They were originally administered by students and shared with students so they could know what they were getting into before registering for classes. Shortly thereafter administrations took control of them, sharing results with faculty—but not with students. The idea was to provide faculty information with which they could improve their teaching. It was not long before administrations began using them as a tool for assessing teaching effectiveness. That is their main function today. As such they impact personnel decisions: who is hired, rehired, given merit raises, and presented with teaching awards. And while faculty can, ostensibly, use the results of student course evaluations to improve their teaching, they are not timely because results are not available until classes are over. Plus, it is sometimes difficult for instructors to decipher student course evaluations (Benton, 2011) and they often do not know how to make the changes called for by students (Centra, 1993).

While students do have something to say about their experience in our classes, and we should listen to them, traditional end-of-course evaluations do not get what adjunct and part-time instructors really need and should want.

What we should want from our students is slow, deliberative responses to the question, "How are things going?" And we should want it in a timely fashion so adjustments can be made along the way. Below are a few suggestions on how to get the information needed from students. Each idea comes from the literature cited (see, for example, Murray, 1985; Koon & Murray, 1995; Witt, Wheeless, & Allen, 2004; Hess, 2006).

Administer a Mid-Course Evaluation
As a department chair I routinely suggested new part-time instructors administer a mid-course evaluation to gauge their performance. Those that did so routinely reported it was a useful exercise. And students appreciate the exercise, too.

What do you ask? I suggest three questions: What is going right in this course? What is going wrong? What can be changed going forward? And do this anonymously.

The benefit is that you learn when something is not going as you think and when there may be time to make adjustments. More importantly, sharing the results with students (during the next class session) shows you care, listen, and are willing to adjust if you can. But be ready: many student suggestions will not be adoptable. Review their suggestions with them and explain why you cannot adopt them for that class at that time—or for any class. You listened; you heard; you cared; you communicated. And you learned something, too.

I do not remember where I read this, but somebody once reported that he administered such an instrument weekly, asking four questions. (1) What stood out as the most significant thing you learned this week? (2) What activities most contributed to your learning? (3) What impeded your learning? (4) If you woke up tomorrow and this course was Great!, if you couldn't wait to come to class tomorrow, if you felt energized thinking about it and preparing for it, what would we have been doing? Notice that for the most part the focus here is on student learning.

Mid-term course evaluations should be a regular part of all classes. The results should be shared with students and with department chairs. With department chairs it is important to mention and discuss what you have done and to report the changes made to the remainder of the class or changes you will make to future iterations of the class as a result of the mid-term course evaluation. That is evidence of good teaching.

Use a Modified SGID
Another way to get useful information from students is the use a modification of a Small Group Instructional Diagnosis (Munro, 2000; White, 2004), also called quality circles (Orts, 1997) and student advisory teams (Hess, 1998). Here is how they work.

Gather a group of five or six students together that are representative of the class. Periodically meet with them as a group, and ask them to provide feedback about your teaching, their classroom experience, and student performance in class. Be sure the rest of the class knows who is part of this group. Encourage the class to bring any problems they have to their representatives.

Meet with this advisory group three or four times during a semester. Focus the discussion on your teaching and classroom dynamics. Take a few minutes at the beginning of the next class session to report the meeting's results. This shows you listen and take student input seriously. Ask the advisory group members about your meeting de-brief.

The purpose of the exercise, which takes both out-of-class and in-class time, is to get input from students about what helps, what hinders, and what they suggest you do to improve their learning. It is all about their learning. Don't be afraid to disagree with student criticisms, but explain your reasons and why you do what you do in the classroom. The purpose of the exercise is to give you an opportunity to make changes along the way that will help students learn. And remember to share the experience with your department chair.

Complete the Current Evaluation Form Yourself

There is zero chance that end-of-course student evaluations will go away, so glean from them what you can. First, fill out the same course evaluation form that students complete. Do it at about the same time they do, but before you receive their responses. Then, when the results are distributed, compare your responses with theirs. Where do you see agreement? Where do you see disagreement? Why might there be a disagreement? Third, when you receive their responses pay particular attention to written comments; they are the most instructive even if many students skip the free-form comments. Finally, reflect on what you learn from this exercise, but do not keep it a secret. Tell your department chair what you have done, what you have learned, and what you plan to adjust about teaching as a result.

Summary

If you want the administration to consider more than end-of-course student evaluations when making decisions that impact you, you have to provide it yourself. The foregoing are suggestions of what you can do, on your own behalf, to improve student learning, your teaching performance, and to present your case to administrators. Your end-of-course student evaluations will likely improve, too.

Some of these suggestions are easy and involve little time or effort; others require significant time and effort. *Each takes student input seriously* yet moves beyond traditional end-of-course surveys of student opinion and satisfaction.

References

Benton, Jr., R. (2011). Using student course evaluations to design faculty development workshops. *Academy of Educational Leadership Journal, 15*(2), 41–53.

Centra, J. A. (1993). *Reflective faculty evaluation: Enhancing teaching and determining faculty effectiveness.* San Francisco: Jossey-Bass Publishers.

Hess, G. F. (1998). Student involvement in improving law teaching and learning. *UMKC Law Review, 67,* 342–366.

Hess, G. F. (2006). Improving teaching and learning in law school: Faculty development research, principles and programs. *Widener Law Review, 12,* 443–471.

Koon, J., & Murray, H. G. (1995). Using multiple outcomes to validate student ratings of overall teacher effectiveness. *Journal of Higher Education, 66*(1), 61–81.

Munro, G. S. (2000). *Outcomes assessment for law schools.* Spokane, Wash.: Institute for Law School Teaching, Gonzaga University School of Law.

Murray, H. G. (1985). Classroom teaching behaviors related to college teaching effectiveness. In J.G. Donald & A.M. Sullivan (Eds.), *Using Research to Improve Teaching.* San Francisco: Jossey-Bass.

Orts, E. W. (1997). Quality circles in law teaching. *Journal of Legal Education, 47*(3), 425–431.

White, K. (2004). Mid-course adjustments: Using small group instructional diagnoses to improve teaching and learning. Retrieved from: http://www.evergreen.edu/washcenter/resources/acl/c4.html

Witt, P. L., Wheeless, L. R., & Allen, M. (2004). A meta-analytical review of the relationship between teacher immediacy and student learning. *Communication Monographs, 71*(2), 184–207.

There is zero chance that end-of-course student evaluations will go away, so glean from them what you can.

The Once and Future King: Adjunct Status and Impact at the American University

Mary A. Cooksey
Indiana University East

Mary (Ange) Cooksey has taught courses at Indiana University since 1986, first as an adjunct instructor, then as a senior lecturer. She has taught for several different regional campuses, and at numerous satellite locations across northeast Indiana.

Keywords: Adjunct History, Organizational Structure, Future of Education, Instruction

Adjunct instruction has a long and rich history in the Academy. From Plato's original school to the university today, part time, temporary teachers have been sharing their vast stores of knowledge, expertise, and gifts with students all over the globe, and doing so without tenure or any promises of permanency in their roles at the universities or colleges at which they work. Their impact has always been great; their status always tenuous. The time has come, however, to rethink what has been the traditional status of adjunct instruction in the Academy as its impact will become greater with increased use due to downsized university budgets, and will grow in scope because of the international explosion in on line delivery of full degree programs.

Historically, thinkers and teachers are people for whom transience has been a natural force with which to engage,

> That permanent faculty burdened with the business of conducting the operations of the university had little time to teach.
>
> • • • • • • • • • • • • •

drawing from its core, fresh perspectives on ideas, issues and critical thinking. Thus, teachers in the earliest educational settings came and went with the ebb and flow of their research and scholarly work. However, with the establishment of the first universities, the assemblage of a faculty became the order of the day, in part because of the religious affiliation and modeling of early schools, but also due to a desire to build permanent structures of human resource in complement to the architectural appeal of the university. What soon became clear, though, was that permanent faculty burdened with the business of conducting the operations of the university had little time to teach. Therefore, in many cases and in many places, actual classroom teaching became a task relegated to visiting lecturers, classroom apprentices, or teaching assistants. Adjunct instruction was re-born.

Due to the subordination that occurred as part of the re-emergence of adjunct instruction, its recent status in the American Academy has been less than desirable. All the while, though, its impact has been growing—both in scope and in depth. Today, most major American universities rely on adjunct instruction for nearly half of all face-to-face and online teaching accomplished each year. This occurs primarily for two reasons: cost and cost. Generally, adjunct instruction is at least one-fourth less expensive than full-time instruction in raw costs—raw costs being defined as dollars actually paid to the adjunct instructor to teach a course or a credit hour. Also, adjunct instruction is one hundred percent cheaper in terms of soft costs—soft costs being defined as expenses like insurance and benefits. For the Academy, adjunct instruction was, and still is, a win-win situation. For adjunct instruction, not so much.

But the tide is turning.

With the advent of eroding tax bases and shrinking university budgets, and with the growth of the delivery of online programs, virtual courses and MOOCS (massive open online courses), administrators have had to find ways to staff ever growing numbers of classes with fewer and fewer dollars. The answer has been reliance upon more and more adjunct instruction, and what is occurring now is just short of a revolution in higher education. The Academy has learned that adjunct instruction is, for the most part, excellent, and is, by content and delivery, most of the time up to par with its full time counterpart. This realization has becomes a fertile starting ground from which to build the sleeker, more cost efficient university of the 21st century—one that is more portable, agile and flexible than ever before. At the core of this new and improved Academy, adjunct instruction…and cost may not be the only reason.

The 21st-century student is someone who needs an eclectic skill set upon graduation, a skill set that will likely be more dependent upon applied knowledge and specialty training, rather than upon depth and breadth of knowledge in Arts and Science or in the Humanities. More than likely, these areas will remain part of a university education; however, in the next decade, the likelihood also is that they will become overshadowed by the need for our work force to be technologically savvy and organizationally skilled. Because of this shift, the need for full-time instruction in these areas will decrease. In turn, the need for adjunct instruction will increase. If this shift expresses itself discipline after discipline and field after field, the scope and impact of adjunct instruction will grow exponentially. And with this growth will come a compelling need to re-think the status of adjunct instruction. Inevitably, adjunct instruction will absorb more and more responsibility for individual course assessment, and with this absorption will come growing responsibility for course revision and new course creation; both will be part of closing the assessment loop. As the adjunct role in these areas proliferates, so will the need for the adjunct instructor's professional development and continuing education. These will combine to increase qualification and credential in adjunct instruction, pushing to the front the need for redefinition of the status of adjunct instruction at the American university.

All of this is good news for the individual visiting lecturer, part-time teacher, or adjunct instructor. Their rightful place at the front table of the Academy will finally be set, and their importance in its life—and in that of students—will be duly recognized. The next challenge will be to ensure that all of the amenities of improved status and recognition follow in the form of higher wages and benefit packages. With optimism, we proceed.

All of this is good news for the individual visiting lecturer, part-time teacher, or adjunct instructor. Their rightful place at the front table of the Academy will finally be set, and their importance in its life—and in that of students—will be duly recognized.

COLLEAGUE OBSERVATION/EVALUATION OF TEACHING: WHO? HOW? WHAT? AND WHAT NEXT?

NATHANAEL G. MITCHELL
SPALDING UNIVERSITY

Dr. Mitchell is an assistant professor in the School of Professional Psychology at Spalding University. He was an adjunct professor himself for 3 years early in his career and is now in a training role mentoring new faculty and lecturers.

AMY FOWKES
SPALDING UNIVERSITY

Dr. Fowkes is an assistant professor at Spalding University with previous experience as a lecturer teaching undergraduate psychology courses.

NORAH C. SLONE
SPALDING UNIVERSITY

Dr. Slone is an assistant professor in the School of Professional Psychology at Spalding University. She has been a lecturer for the past year and received invaluable mentorship from a co-author on the paper.

JONATHAN CARRIER
LARAMIE COUNTY COMMUNITY COLLEGE

Jonathan Carrier is the department chair of Math and Sciences at the Albany County Campus of Laramie County Community College and has been a psychology instructor for the past eight years. As part of this position, Jonathan supervises numerous adjunct faculty in History, Sociology, Psychology, Mathematics, and a variety of science courses.

Keywords: Teaching Evaluation, Teaching Effectiveness, Colleague Feedback, Colleague Observation/Evaluation of Teaching: Who? How? What? and What Next, Peer Review

Framework

From our experience, having an expert teacher observe/evaluate our teaching has been one of the most beneficial and simultaneously most anxiety provoking aspects of professional development as adjunct or new instructors. While an invitation to teach as an adjunct or lecturer is generally flattering, it also means being immersed in an unfamiliar process. Many universities do not offer trainings of best practices in teaching and rarely inform new adjunct hires of expectations regarding teaching performance. This environment often leads to a general sense of uncertainty and little opportunity for skill development for the new adjunct professor. Having a colleague observe and evaluate your teaching provides objective evidence regarding strengths and growth areas for professional development.

Engaging a faculty member that is well respected among colleagues

Making it Work

Who? Engaging a faculty member that is well respected among colleagues as an "expert teacher" is likely who you want to seek out. As such, finding those who publish in the scholarship of teaching and learning literature may be a good place to start. Additionally, if you are teaching at a large institution, there may be centers of teaching and learning that would have recommendations of faculty for you. Further, we recommend asking students in your classes which professors at your institution have inspired them and why? The professors who are regularly inspiring their students are the colleagues from whom you want to learn. Finally, you will want to pick a colleague who will be able to communicate the results of the observation in a manner that will be helpful. Colleagues whom you observe to be critical of others or not able to present ideas in a balanced and palatable manner should be avoided for this task. You do not want to purse a colleague who will only tell you how wonderfully you are doing and not provide areas for growth. Someone who is able to provide you honest feedback that motivates and ultimately leads to development is the person to ask.

How? After you have an idea of whom you would like to observe your teaching, the next step is to ask. Fortunately, those of us who have a passion for excellence in teaching often love to assist colleagues in getting excited about good teaching as well. Therefore, it is rare that we will say "no" to your request and have very likely participated in the process many times ourselves. However, you will want to make sure that your colleague has enough time and desire to complete the observation. As such, you want to provide the request for observation well in advance of the lecture/class you would like for them to observe. It is critical that you establish with your colleague an agreed-upon template or goals for the observation. Vague parameters and unclear areas of assessment only increase the anxiety already present in abundance.

What? The peer review is generally a one-class observation of teaching skills conducted in the actual classroom setting. However, the in-class observation is not always possible due to logistical barriers. Providing a colleague with a video recording of classroom teaching is a viable alternative. The colleague reviewer is able to observe the faculty member conducting a demonstration of the goals and objectives for the lesson. Helpful format objectives for the observation/evaluation may include:
- Class Pacing
- Presentation Style
- Classroom Activities

- Use of Technology
- Student Engagement
- Assessment of Student Learning
- Class Management Techniques
- Course Syllabus
- General Summary of Strengths of the Instructor
- Recommendations for Improvement

Specific topics/objectives for the evaluation will depend on adjunct goals, experience, and content of the course.

Future Implications

What next? Let's be honest, most of us do not like hearing about what we need to improve upon. Even if we are dedicated to professional development, constructive feedback can still "sting a little." Therefore, after the formal observation has been completed, take a deep breath and congratulate yourself for caring enough about your students' learning that you are seeking this level of feedback.

We suggest that you ask your colleague to provide a copy of their evaluation to you in advance of in-person feedback. This will allow you to privately process the results as well as develop questions for the colleague based on his/her recommendations for your growth. An in-person follow-up meeting to discuss the results of the observation/evaluation is also recommended. There are times that how something is said in person leads to a more positive outcomes than how it is interpreted by the reader. Again, if you choose the right colleague to complete the observation, they will be sensitive to your current development as an instructor and excited to share specific ways to improve. It may even be helpful to ask them about their first peer observation and the most important advice they've received regarding improving instruction. The entire process, if designed effectively, can be an avenue to improved teaching and personal growth.

After the formal observation has been completed, take a deep breath and congratulate yourself for caring enough about your students' learning that you are seeking this level of feedback.

Writing with Familiarity: Comfortable or Trite?

Leslie Elrod
University of Cincinnati, Blue Ash College

Dr. Elrod was an adjunct and teaching fellow for many years before becoming a tenured faculty member. She continues to mentor adjuncts and teaching fellows in developing their careers and job prospects.

Keywords: Writing, Professional Development

Framework

Landing a position as an adjunct or lecturer in a tight market requires a competitive portfolio with an emphasis on strong publications that relate to your field. Adjuncts and lecturers are often employed at multiple locations which makes it difficult to find the time to do research and write.

Thus there is a temptation to often keep restating the same material with a new title. When choosing topics on which to write, familiarity can be comfortable and reassuring, but familiarity can also be trite. This may be a comfortable route but resume reviewers will immediately realize that the topic is overused and the applicant is just re-presenting the same data with a new title. What else can be said about a topic about which you've written/presented for several years?

Making it Work

What to do? If you haven't completely exhausted all there is to be said by you about the topic, try a new venue. If you always seek publication in trade journals, such as English-language journals, go broader to include language-arts journals (or vice versa). If you have completely exhausted your topic, then try to take a new angle. Go back to the literature and rethink your idea. Of course, it is best to try a new topic and show your versatility. Take a new angle that necessitates going back to the literature. Better yet, try a new topic, whether related or completely different.

In addition to reviewing the bibliographies of works related to your topic of interest check out university presses, such as Oxford University Press (2014). A general search for academic journals may lead to publishing outlets that you had not previously considered. For example, Scientific and Academic Publishing (2014) is an open-access (unrestricted access and reuse) publishing resource. When seeking to publish in open-access resources, beware of pay to publish since a resume reviewer might question the validity of the journal and its peer review process. Stick with mainstream journals that are peer reviewed (Beall, 2014).

In my experience on hiring committees, a strong publication record, even though not often required for adjuncts and lecturers, can set you apart, showing interest and dedication to the discipline as well as to teaching. The topics of your research can add depth to classroom discussion and content.

Future Implications

Trying to write about a new topic is daunting but it will pay off in the hiring process. It will also inspire your creative muse and make the research and writing process exciting again. Not only will bucking familiarity refresh your perspective but will strengthen your C.V. and career prospects.

References

Beall, J. (2014). List of predatory publishers 2014 [Web log post]. Retrieved from: http://scholarlyoa.com/2014/01/02/list-of-predatory-publishers-2014/.

Oxford Journals (2014). Retrieved from: http://www.oxfordjournals.org/.

Scientific and Academic Publishing (2014). Retrieved from: http://www.sapub.org/journal/alljournalslist.aspx.

Take a new angle that necessitates going back to the literature.
Better yet, try a new topic, whether related or completely different.

Faculty's Concerns Regarding Adapting Technological Advances to Reach Pedagogical Goals

Jessie Reed
Spalding University

Jessie Reed is a doctoral student at Spalding University in the clinical psychology program. Her graduate assistantship focuses on helping train, mentor and otherwise prepare full-time and part-time faculty to successfully teach online.

DeDe Wohlfarth
Spalding University

DeDe Wohlfarth is a full-time faculty member at Spalding University who is still semi-clueless in teaching online, despite having made significant gains in doing so.

Keywords: Technology, Pedagogy, Faculty Development

Advances in technology have impacted almost all parts of modern society, creating new and more sophisticated tools and methods to better achieve goals. Our classrooms are no exceptions. However, maximizing the benefits of such advances require proper training. A survey of faculty at a private university in the Midwest investigated faculty opinions toward and confidence with new technology. With a notably high completion rate of 77%, including many part-time faculty responding, the survey results suggested that 75% of participants had at least one concern regarding online teaching. The most often selected concern was "I don't know how to coordinate the pedagogical application with the technology means/methods." Such a concern indicates that faculty may lack training in selecting and applying technological advances to successful teaching practices that have worked for them in their face-to-face classes.

> Fortunately, strides in technology make such adaptation possible.

Classroom techniques that faculty endorsed using "frequently" included: using student assessment data to evaluate instruction, using group work/group projects, creating assignments that have multiple solutions, and designing highly interactive courses between instructor and students. Teaching skills, such as those listed above, are often utilized in face-to-face classroom settings, but as online and hybrid courses become more common in higher education, faculty must find ways in which to adapt their learning strategies to platforms other than physical classrooms.

Fortunately, strides in technology make such adaptation possible. Google Drive, for example, is a useful tool that approximates several of the above-mentioned teaching techniques, including using group work/group projects, creating assignments that have multiple solutions, and designing highly interactive courses. Google Drive is a free cloud storage service that allows users to create, edit, and share collaborative documents online. Google Drive allows students working on group projects to do so remotely in real time and provides many tools which promote interaction between students and professors. Unfortunately, despite being relatively user friendly, 32% of survey respondents were unaware of what Google Drive is, while 27% responded that they wished to utilize the tool, but did not know how. These results suggest that more than half of participating instructors would be unable to properly execute using the tool without additional training.

Of course, Google Drive is only one example of dozens of technological tools that may be used to improve pedagogy. The sheer amount of available tools is in fact an issue, as some faculty may feel overwhelmed by determining what the "right" technology is to promote their pedagogical goals. Educators need training in how to choose technology that is aligned with their course goals, framework, and student academic and technological skills level and resources. No easy flowchart answers these questions, and the most-cited barriers to implementing change emerge again: a lack of money (on behalf of universities) and time (on behalf of faculty). Addressing these realistic concerns is paramount to ensure the best-quality learning experiences are created for students.

PEER REVIEW: IT'S NOT JUST FOR TENURE

ROBIN K. MORGAN
INDIANA UNIVERSITY SOUTHEAST

Robin is currently a professor of psychology and serves as the university director of the Faculty Colloquium on Excellence in Teaching. As a graduate student, she also taught as an adjunct faculty member at a community college.

Keywords: Peer Review, Promotion, Formative, Summative

In recent years, increasing numbers of faculty have begun availing themselves of systematic peer review to improve their teaching and to document excellence in teaching. Systematic peer review can be of great benefit as it allows faculty to identify opportunities for improving their teaching and to have a peer comment on their teaching. Such peer reviews can be of significant benefit when approaching tenure or promotion.

Adjunct faculty and lecturers have been less likely to jump on the peer review bandwagon. This is unfortunate as peer review can provide many of the same benefits to these faculty. That is, a peer review can assist in improving teaching thereby enhancing student learning. The effort expended in peer review is seen by those who are hiring adjunct faculty and lecturers in a positive manner. As universities increase the number of adjuncts and lecturers hired, competition may also increase for these positions. Having a documented history of peer review suggests to those hiring for these positions that this is a person who cares about their teaching and has taken steps to improve.

Before jumping into peer review, though, it is important to understand the different types of peer review. Many universities will offer two types of peer review: formative and summative. Formative peer reviews are a low-risk form of peer review. Formative peer review is designed solely to improve teaching and the goal is to develop recommendations for improvement. The process is confidential between the peer reviewer and the person requesting the peer review. Typically, a peer review report is produced and provided to the person requesting the peer review. Summative peer reviews involve evaluation. That is, in a summative review, the goal is to evaluate how well the person is teaching. In many cases, this means that a peer review report will be written with an evaluation at the end of the report. The level of confidentiality in a summative review is typically not as tight as for a formative review. The report that is written as a result of a summative review is frequently shared with the department chair, dean, or other person designated by the person being reviewed.

These differences are important. If your goal is to improve your teaching, requesting a formative peer review would be a logical first step. Since the resulting report will be given only to the person requesting the review, this would allow you the greatest flexibility in using the recommendations for future improvement. You can also include sections of the report to document your commitment to teaching.

Formative peer reviews are a low-risk form of peer review. Formative peer review is designed solely to improve teaching and the goal is to develop recommendations for improvement. The process is confidential between the peer reviewer and the person requesting the peer review.

GETTING REAL ABOUT MENTORSHIP

NORAH C. SLONE
SPALDING UNIVERSITY

Dr. Slone is an assistant professor in the School of Professional Psychology at Spalding University. She has been a lecturer for the past year and received invaluable mentorship from a co-author on the paper.

NATHANAEL G. MITCHELL
SPALDING UNIVERSITY

Dr. Mitchell is an assistant professor in the School of Professional Psychology at Spalding University. He was an adjunct professor himself for 3 years early in his career and is now in a training role mentoring new faculty and lecturers.

JONATHAN CARRIER
LARAMIE COUNTY COMMUNITY COLLEGE

Jonathan Carrier is the department chair of Math and Sciences at the Albany County Campus of Laramie County Community College and has been a psychology instructor for the past eight years. As part of this position, Jonathan supervises numerous adjunct faculty in History, Sociology, Psychology, Mathematics, and a variety of science courses.

BARBARA BEAUCHAMP
SPALDING UNIVERSITY

Dr. Beauchamp is an associate professor at Spalding University. Mentorship as both mentee and mentor has greatly contributed to her understanding of pedagogy, distance education, and human diversity.

Keywords: Mentoring, Professional Development, Faculty Development

Framework

Most of us would not be where we are without effective mentoring. Becoming an effective instructor in higher education requires guidance along the way. Academic mentorship has been touted as an effective method for promoting success across fields of study (Kohn, 2014); however, less is written about the process of developing and utilizing meaningful mentorship. Working with our mentors and mentees over the years has afforded us several opportunities to reflect on what constitutes effective mentorship.

Research defines mentorship as "someone of more advanced rank or experience who guides, teaches, and develops a novice" (Zerzan, Hess, Schur, Phillips, & Rigotti, 2009, p. 140). Literature suggests that mentorship has a number of benefits, including learning how to organize the complexities associated with beginning an adjunct position along with increased career satisfaction, self-confidence in professional development, productivity, and sense of community (Carey & Weissman, 2010; Sorcilleni, 1994).

While the aforementioned benefits are important, new and adjunct faculty members often have emotional reactions and questions related to the process of teaching in higher education that can be difficult to manage. Such questions reflect an emotional pressure that occurs on top of the busyness of teaching, such as, "Am I going to be good enough?" "Why aren't my students performing as well as I expected?" "Will I be effective, liked, and successful enough to get a renewed contract?" There are few places in academia where being real about emotionally vulnerable questions is safe or wise. However, with the right mentor(s), it is possible to not only address the pragmatic questions related to effective teaching practices and classroom management, but also a place to genuinely address insecurities that most all beginning instructors and adjuncts hold.

Making it Work

1. **Find the right mentor for you.** Some adjuncts are automatically paired with mentors; however, that person may or may not be a mentor with whom you

feel safe enough to discuss insecurities. If that person is not the right fit, it may be helpful to: a) evaluate whether providing feedback to your mentor may adjust the process enough for you to feel comfortable, or b) seek out an additional mentor on your own with whom you can discuss more vulnerable areas of your experience.

2. **Challenge yourself to take emotional risks once you find a mentor with whom you feel safe**. For example, from our experience, it was normalizing for the mentee to be able to say, "I didn't know how to answer a student's question in class this week, and I felt embarrassed and incompetent," and the mentee's statement be answered with a normalizing comment that suggested even experienced faculty feel the same way from time to time. Feeling less alone and ashamed in our responses to the all-too-frequent emotional reactions to teaching can be invaluable.

3. **Invest in mentorship on a routine basis (e.g., weekly)**. If you are able, preschedule mentoring meetings in advance for a set time/date for the entire semester. All of us in academia feel "too busy sometimes," but without adequate support, we can find ourselves floundering quickly. Therefore, do everything in your power to not reschedule or cancel the meetings once they are in your calendar. As a new adjunct, there will be times that feel overwhelming with questions on what would be best from either a classroom management or effective teaching perspective. It can be helpful to meet on a weekly basis to discuss the options for how to respond to particular situations that arise or to brainstorm teaching methods/pedagogical techniques for the next class session. Knowing such support was routine felt reassuring and comforting when we (the authors) were mentees.

4. **Develop goals for yourself.** Having one or two professional or teaching goals for yourself may focus the overall direction of mentoring beyond the structural needs that often occur, such as how to input grades, or where to locate teaching resources. For example, one of my [NS] goals for the year was to increase my knowledge and effective application of evidence-based teaching practices. Informing your mentor of said goals may provide support that is most directly tailored to your needs.

5. **Ask your mentor to help you develop additional goals.** Developing goals for yourself is a great way to stay motivated and accountable to growth throughout the semester. However, all of us have "blind spots" regarding skills. Put another way, "we don't know what we don't know." Having a more experienced colleague gently offer potential goals that we have not considered (maybe something related from their observations of our skills or something that was helpful in their development) could make the difference from being "good to great."

6. **Check in on the mentoring process routinely.** Reviewing the effectiveness of the mentorship process can be a way to ensure that mentees' goals are being met and progress is being made in a way that feels most supportive. For example, if your mentor is less structured than you may prefer, or meetings feel less organized, it may be helpful to advocate for the topics you most need to address from the outset. We [NM and NS] found it helpful to start the meeting with an agenda to ensure that the most pressing needs were reviewed, to use the time we had most efficiently. Additionally, in our experience, there was often a check-in process at the end of mentoring meetings, to evaluate what was most helpful or what else was needed that was not addressed during the hour.

Future Implications

It is our hope that adjunct faculty will find effective support through mentorship using these tips. High quality mentorship can provide not only structural support on how to develop effective teaching skills, but also for the genuine emotional experiences that accompany the beginning of a new teaching position. It is our experience that gaining support in effectively managing our personal reactions to teaching in addition to honing pedagogical skills led to more positive learning outcomes for both our students and ourselves as beginning instructors.

References

Carey, E. C., & Weissman, D. E. (2010). Understanding and finding mentorship: A review for junior faculty. *Journal of Palliative Medicine, 13*, 1373–1379. doi: 10.1089/jpm.2010.0091

Kohn, H. (2014). A mentoring program to help junior faculty members achieve scholarship success. *American Journal of Pharmaceutical Education, 78*, 1–6. doi: 10.5688/ajpe78229

Sorcinelli, M. D. (1994). Effective approaches to new faculty development. *Journal of Counseling and Development, 72*, 474–479. doi: 10.1002/j.1556-6676.1994.tb00976.x

Zerzan, J. T., Hess, R., Schur, E., Phillips, R. S., & Rigotti, N. (2009). Making the most of mentors: A guide for mentees. *Academic Medicine, 84*, 140–144. doi:10.1097/ACM.0b013e3181906e8f

ON BEING "ROOTED" IN THE CLASSROOM: TOP THREE TEACHING TIPS FROM "THE BAREFOOT PROFESSOR"

SHARILYNN ROBINSON-LYNK
UNIVERSITY OF MICHIGAN

ShariLynn Robinson-Lynk, LMSW, ACSW, is a Lecturers' Employee Organization adjunct lecturer at the University of Michigan, Ann Arbor, MI School of Social Work. She was also recently nominated by the students as the 2014 Professor of the Year for the School of Social Work.

Keywords: Connection, Environment, Professional Development Path, Career Path

I must begin by clarifying that while I do indeed often teach without my shoes, I am not at all suggesting this as a teaching tip! However, there is a connection. What I am suggesting as my first teaching tip is that every instructor must find some way to be "rooted," or connected if you will, to her/his students. None of the following tips, nor any other's you may read I dare to say, will be successful if the students do not feel you are invested and concerned about their learning journey.

One of the many ways in which students have shared with me that they know I am invested in their learning, which also often times includes creating a safe (even if not always comfortable!) environment is that I always share my teaching journey. It is this expression of vulnerability and trust that opens up the classroom for mutual sharing and growth. It is with my teaching journey that I will begin this article.

It was towards the end of a successful fifteen-year professional social work career that I unexpectedly stumbled onto an opportunity to present a guest lecture on living and working in the profession with multiple intersecting identities to a class of social work students. After the lecture, the professor of the class (herself, "barefoot" literally, as well as figuratively, as far as I could assess!) offered to walk me out of the class and immediately announced that I needed to be teaching! Though I had never entertained the idea, I felt the pull that afternoon. The very next semester I was not only guest lecturing again in her class, but also co-teaching a class with her. When an adjunct teaching position became available the following semester, with her guidance, I applied and accepted the offer to begin my teaching career.

She was my instant mentor and I taught at that university for over five years. Rewardingly enough, I experienced all of these wonderful opportunities at my graduate school alma mater. I later went on to teach social work courses for three additional local universities and introductory anthropology courses for the local community college before my arrival at

the University of Michigan in 2010. Needless to say, teaching is not just a profession for me. I feel quite confident and comfortable saying I *am* a teacher and I happen to also have the joy and honor of doing so for a living.

Since I have always been quite fascinated with improving my teaching skills, my teaching journey also included some time working in the area of the scholarship of teaching and learning. It was during that time that I became aware of several pedagogies which I found fit my need to be "rooted" in the classroom and vulnerable with the students; or, as students have often said to me, "real." These include all of Paulo Freire's pedagogies, especially his work on critical pedagogies. Highly recommended readings on these critical pedagogies which have been particularly moving and integrative to my teaching have been, Pedagogy of Love, which is a compilation of Freire's pedagogies by one of his protégé's, Antonia Darder. bell hooks' trio of teaching wisdom which includes, Teaching to Transgress: *Education as the Practice of Freedom; Teaching Community: A Pedagogy of Hope and Teaching Critical Thinking: Practical Wisdom* are also highly recommended readings.

While Paulo Freire is known for much pedagogy, it was the critical lens in which he viewed the educational system, terming it a, "banking" method and advocating instead for a liberationist educational system, which greatly influences my teaching.

Thus, my second teaching tip, is to, whenever possible, encourage critical thinking and reflection and to teach through dialogue. However, to do so, we must first prepare our students through a series of experiences which will have them reminisce and remember, then acknowledge, that their previous educational experiences (most likely!) included them passively having information "deposited" into their brains and then during test-taking time being told to "withdraw" the information; all of this with the absence of critical thinking or praxis. Once we have tackled this acknowledgement, the skill of dialogue, which also includes defining how these are different from, and connected to, debate, discourse and discussions, can then be taught and applied.

Though last, my final teaching tip is one in which I would say guides the previous two tips. I strongly believe that being rooted while expressing vulnerability and trust and encouraging critical thinking through dialogue cannot be successful without the presence of love. Once we have the good fortune of graduating from kindergarten where words and deeds of affection are not only taught and encouraged, but

expected, we tend to focus on love in its purely romantic and sexual sense. I maintain that a genuine sense of caring and concern and connectedness to our students will go a long way in assisting them with successfully integrating all of the content and learning outcomes we are required to ensure that they have.

Best wishes to all who read this and to our students.

Love,
Shari

Taking your Professional Development on the Road

Jon Becker
INDIANA UNIVERSITY NORTHWEST

Jon Becker is a senior lecturer at Indiana University Northwest in the Department of Mathematics and Actuarial Science. He is also a former high school math teacher. Mr. Becker has been recognized for teaching excellence through his membership in the Faculty Colloquium on Excellence in Teaching (FACET) as well as numerous campus and system wide teaching awards. Jon devotes his professional service to developing resources for adjunct faculty and lecturers and serves as the chair for the planning of the annual FALCON event, a nationwide, professional teaching conference for adjunct faculty and lecturers.

Keywords: Professional Development, Conferences, FALCON, Lilly Conferences, Centers for Teaching and Learning

As the numbers of adjunct faculty members swell across the United States, the need for high-quality professional growth opportunities increases as well. Many new adjuncts are content area specialists who may have little to no prior teaching experience. As such, they face an unfamiliar landscape of responsibilities for which they ae likely poorly prepared. Classroom management, syllabi design, test preparation and administration, and even interactions with other colleagues are just a few unfamiliar areas for many new adjunct faculty members. Throwing a content area expert with little teaching experience into the classroom without any support and expecting them to "sink or swim" is unfair to the instructor and potentially damaging to their students.

Universities have started to recognize that new adjunct faculty members need mentoring and development opportunities which have previously been geared largely toward full-time faculty. Many campus centers for teaching and learning (CTLs) now offer orientation workshops for all new faculty members and also open up professional development opportunities to adjunct faculty members as well as the full-time faculty for whom they are usually designed.

Still, this isn't always enough. By the nature of their schedules, adjunct faculty members often feel isolated, frequently teaching in the evening or on weekends when most other department members are not on campus. The opportunities offered by the CTLs may not be provided at times conducive to the adjunct's full-time work schedule.

Teaching conferences offer a tremendous opportunity for professional growth.

Teaching conferences offer a tremendous opportunity for professional growth. *The Lilly Conferences on College Teaching and Learning* are offered annually at a variety of locations across the United States. With conferences in Michigan, Washington, DC, California, Ohio, and North Carolina, there is a Lilly near everyone. Participation is not regional, and not every conference is identical, so there are a variety of opportunities for professional growth. Faculty members of all ranks are invited and encouraged to attend.

Indiana University holds an annual conference geared specifically for adjunct faculty and non-tenured full-time faculty members. FALCON (FACET's Adjunct Faculty and Lecturers Conference) is held every fall. This conference tailors its programming, including all workshops, poster sessions, roundtable discussions, and keynote speakers, to address the specific and unique needs of part-time and non-tenure track faculty members. FALCON's Mission Statement is as follows:

> FALCON exists to provide a forum for non-tenured lecturers and adjunct instructors from all disciplines to exchange academic and professional development strategies designed to enhance teaching and student learning in the classroom.

Open to participants from across the country, FALCON's unique focus on the most rapidly growing population of instructors in higher education provides a can't miss networking and development option for those adjunct faculty members focused on professional growth.

Whether through campus CTLs or teaching conferences, there is a mounting need for professional development for part-time faculty. Across the United State, estimates suggest that only 27 percent of college instructors are full-time tenured or tenure track; the remaining 73 percent are adjuncts and non-tenured lecturers. As more universities recognize this, resources for adjunct professional development are becoming more readily available. However, the availability of these resources may not be communicated well. As instructors, it is incumbent upon us to reach out to our campus CTLs to see what resources may be available to help us grow.

References

The Lilly Conferences on College Teaching and Learning Home Page. Retrieved from: http://lillyconferences.com/

FALCON Home Page. Retrieved from: https://facet.indiana.edu/events-programs/FALCON/index.shtml

Stainburn, S. (2010, January 3). The case of the vanishing full-time professor. *The New York Times*. Retrieved from: http://www.nytimes.com

Across the United State, estimates suggest that only
27 percent of college instructors are full-time tenured or tenure track;
the remaining 73 percent are adjuncts and non-tenured lecturers.
As more universities recognize this, resources for adjunct
professional development are becoming more readily available.

DEVELOPING EFFECTIVE SYLLABI: KEY POINTS FOR NEW INSTRUCTORS

NATHANAEL G. MITCHELL
SPALDING UNIVERSITY

Dr. Mitchell is an assistant professor in the School of Professional Psychology at Spalding University. He was an adjunct professor himself for 3 years early in his career and is now in a training role mentoring new faculty and lecturers.

AMY FOWKES
SPALDING UNIVERSITY

Dr. Fowkes is an assistant professor at Spalding University with previous experience as a lecturer teaching undergraduate psychology courses.

NORAH C. SLONE
SPALDING UNIVERSITY

Dr. Slone is an assistant professor in the School of Professional Psychology at Spalding University. She has been a lecturer for the past year and received invaluable mentorship from a co-author on the paper.

JONATHAN CARRIER
LARAMIE COUNTY COMMUNITY COLLEGE

Jonathan Carrier is the department chair of Math and Sciences at the Albany County Campus of Laramie County Community College and has been a psychology instructor for the past eight years. As part of this position, Jonathan supervises numerous adjunct faculty in History, Sociology, Psychology, Mathematics, and a variety of science courses.

Keywords: Syllabus, Faculty Development

Framework

First impressions matter! For many students, your syllabus is the first impression they have and may influence student perception of the course (Saville, Zinn, Brown, & Marchuk, 2010). Consider carefully the overt and subtle messages that you want to communicate to students. Your syllabus in a wonderful opportunity to immediately and succinctly communicate your passion for the subject, your love of teaching, your philosophy on learning, your expectations, and the relevance of the subject matter to students' lives.

Making it Work

First, consider the tone in which the syllabus will be written. A syllabus infused with creativity, passion, respect, and fairness can create an expectation that the course will be couched in a positive learning environment

Next, we mentally divide our syllabi according to three elements, the academic, institutional, and emotional.

Conceptualizing the purpose of the syllabus in this manner facilitates the creation of a document that is more inclusive and organized.

The academic portion of the syllabus outlines student learning objectives, required assignments and readings, class schedule, and the modes of instruction utilized in the course. It is vital that you communicate that you have been purposeful in determining highly relevant course goals and assignments and have developed fair methods of assessment to evaluate progress towards those goals.

> First impressions matter! ...your syllabus is the first impression they have and may influence student perception of the course

The institutional portion of the syllabus defines the departmental, university, and legal regulations. Policies about academic integrity, support for disability accommodations, respect for differing opinions, office hours, communication standards, late assignments, and withdrawal procedures are examples of institutional constructs. It can be easy with these portions to write in a cold and potentially punitive manner. Being careful to communicate respect, fairness, support, and high expectations aids in positively impacting student perceptions of the course.

The final aspect of the syllabus is the emotional element of the document which utilizes action verbs, first-person or "I" language, highlights creative modes of instruction, and communicates the positive expectations of the instructor. Students can be encouraged to engage in the examination of the discipline, and to enjoy the process of learning. Including your favorite quotes, teaching philosophy, clip art, and aspects of your personal life that may help students to see you as a real person (not just an ivory tower academic) are helpful strategies to breathe life and emotion into your syllabus. Faculty members are powerful role models in the classroom and the syllabus is a written representation of your values.

Future Implications

These recommended strategies can be a helpful model for designing a syllabus that is both flexible and creative. Ideally, the syllabus is more than just a contract between the faculty member and the student. An effective syllabus communicates passion, respect, expectations, and a clear map of the learning outcomes. If you would like to learn more about developing effective syllabi or would like to examine peer-reviewed exemplary syllabi, we encourage you to explore APA Division 2, Society for the Teaching of Psychology, Project Syllabus website at http://teachpsych.org/otrp/syllabi/index.php.

References

Saville, B. K., Zinn, T. W., Brown, A. R., & Marchuk, K. A. (2010). Syllabus detail and students' perceptions of teacher effectiveness. *Teaching of Psychology*, 37, 186–189, doi: 10.1080/00986283.2010.488523

AM I A GOOD TEACHER? WHAT DO MY EVALUATIONS SAY?

MARY EMBRY
INDIANA UNIVERSITY

Mary is a full-time senior lecturer, who has instructed 10 different courses in Apparel Merchandising and Design in the last 13 years.

Keywords: Professional Development, Evaluation

Framework

I have yet to meet an instructor who receives end-of-semester teaching evaluation reports with blatant enthusiasm. Opening student course evaluations is like reading the reviews after the opening of a show. We brace ourselves: did the critics like me? I typically begin with the harbinger what did they like least? Give me the bad news, so I can start to position my teaching ego in front of the least-flattering comments.

For non-tenure track faculty, teaching is the primary role. Unfortunately the mindful review of NTT faculty by peers, superiors, and teaching professionals is often lost in the maintenance of the many moving pieces of an academic program. Student perceptions become the performance review each semester, yet these bits of analysis by young adults present shared confusions: what are we being measured against? What do these numbers mean and to whom should they compared? Am I a good teacher if my students like me?

Making it work

In responding to variables like discipline, student age, class size, and institution, instructors develop a particular style, using a portfolio of methods that address student learning. I have experimentally worked with teaching methods that were subsequently rejected. In this rejection, patterns appeared that pointed to my identity as a teacher. Adopted teaching methods synthesized with my evolving teaching philosophy became the basis of my teaching statement but also the context for student evaluations. Teaching evaluations should be contextualized by the story that is created though the process of learning to teach, acknowledging that good teaching involves application, practice, and reflection.

How teachers compare to every other teacher, or how one compares to the "mean" in some context, is much less valuable to career progression than how student evaluations empower us to tell our story as a teacher. Defining the unique qualities you develop in your teaching practice can be used to identify evaluation items that best measure those qualities. These evaluation items then can be used as evidence, that indeed, you are the teacher you desire to be.

Many of the courses I instruct are focused on conceptual learning, but my courses are often evaluated in light of a core curriculum within a professional program weighted toward procedure-based skill application. As a result, my teaching strategies evolved into use of methods that emphasize relevance. The strategies I adopted addressed finding authentic conceptual applications and making connections between course concepts and students' experiences.

The departmental evaluations are standardized for all instructors. Within these prompts, I identified questions related to "enthusiasm and intellectual stimulation" as most applicable to my intent to teach using applied relevance of concepts, specifically. Thus the prompts inspired interest in content and asks challenging questions became important markers of my success in incorporating "relevance" into my teaching strategies. These questions became the responses I charted from year to year, and because of the particular focus on these items as indicators of relevance, they improved as I refined effective strategies.

I do not explicitly present the fine points of my teaching philosophy to students, as they soon are immersed in the experience of it. Encouraging students to write about their classroom experience has, somewhat unexpectedly, provided the best confirmation that my teaching strategies reach students as intended. A statement such as "I could leave the classroom with something to talk about with my friends" is not just confirmation of engaging topics but demonstrates my ability to make material relevant. Most recently a student wrote:

> "I liked how relevant the material was not only to my major, but to the real world. It was taught in a way that explained potentially confusing topics in an understandable way. I have already began to participate in conversations with adults and students alike about international trade topics"

There have been times in my career when I felt no control over what the final numbers say about the course, where achievement was simply completing the material and grading without anyone slipping off the deep end. It has helped me to not seek perfection in every evaluative prompt, but to tie evaluation with what matters to me as a teacher, and to synthesize those elements into a story describing my teaching. Thus, the story of my professional development and who I am as a teacher becomes concise, easy to share, and clear regarding what differentiates my courses.

Future implications

It may be difficult to influence or change what superiors choose to look at as evidence of teaching. Frequently instructors need to work within the constraints of standardized evaluations and sets of one-dimensional evaluative criteria. There are still opportunities to assess particular methods through the development of pre- and post-course tests or to source assessments from colleagues that share your teaching focus areas. For example, when I began focusing on information literacy, I implemented online pre- and post-tests to shape my teaching methodology. In another instance, when I was looking at internationalization of my curriculum, I worked with an on-campus resource to access a Globalized Perspectives Inventory. There is opportunity to be proactive about influencing the definition and validation of your work as teacher. Opening 'end-of-course' evaluations becomes better positioned as an effort of discovery, instead of a sting of critique, when you begin by asking the right questions of those evaluations.

It may be difficult to influence or change what superiors choose to look at as evidence of teaching. There are still opportunities to assess particular methods through the development of pre- and post-course tests or to source assessments from colleagues that share your teaching focus areas.

PREPARING YOUR COURSE BEFORE THE SEMESTER BEGINS: LESSONS LEARNED THE HARD WAY

JONATHAN CARRIER
LARAMIE COUNTY COMMUNITY COLLEGE

Jonathan Carrier is the department chair of Math and Sciences at the Albany County Campus of Laramie County Community College and has been a psychology instructor for the past eight years. As part of this position, Jonathan supervises numerous adjunct faculty in History, Sociology, Psychology, Mathematics, and a variety of science courses.

NATHANAEL G. MITCHELL
SPALDING UNIVERSITY

Dr. Mitchell is an assistant professor in the School of Professional Psychology at Spalding University. He was an adjunct professor himself for 3 years early in his career and is now in a training role mentoring new faculty and lecturers.

NORAH C. SLONE
SPALDING UNIVERSITY

Dr. Slone is an assistant professor in the School of Professional Psychology at Spalding University. She has been a lecturer for the past year and received invaluable mentorship from a co-author on the paper.

Keywords: Course Preparation, Course Organization, Faculty Development

Framework

Lessons about course organization and preparation often are learned the hard way and at unexpected moments. At some point in their careers, even experienced instructors may have received the dreaded feedback that "my instructor seemed disorganized and scattered" or "classes were too unstructured." Responses like these are not enjoyable to hear but may alert us to a need for further organization and planning, knowing that the extent to which a course is well organized can greatly impact its success or failure (Goos & Hughes, 2000). Considerations for course organization may be found in scheduling the course structure, making preparations, and in implementing the structure with students.

Making it Work

Three primary considerations for course organization are recommended while making preparations. First, if possible, it is recommended that instructors create their entire course before the semester starts (Stark, 2000). This includes preparing, lesson plans, PowerPoints and lectures, handouts, homework assignments, tests, and test study guides. Although it is a significant amount of work up front, doing so will pay off in stress reduction for the instructor and increase the instructor's confidence and course quality once the semester starts.

Second, it is important to consider due dates. Important guidelines may be as follows: a) Provide assignments well in advance. Many effective instructors are in the habit of providing all course homework, assignments, and test study guides in their respective online learning management systems at the beginning of the course. This will assuage many student concerns and fears concerning assignments. b) Create due dates that give students ample time between assignments. This allows students to not only plan when to do assignments for a specific instructor, but also to consider how their time can be best spent working on assignments for their other classes as well. c) Instructors should create due dates across all of their courses at the same time to avoid overloading themselves with grading. Many instructors have made the mistake of assigning due dates for papers and/or midterms at the same time, which results in massive grading responsibilities. Third, it is imperative that instructors provide clear guidelines and rubrics for each subjectively graded assignment (Arter & McTighe, 2001). Rubrics not only help instructors grade with more speed and accuracy, providing them also helps students to understand expectations for their work and a rationale for their grade.

Preparing an in-class "schedule" based on your lesson plan for each class session where possible can create a smooth agenda that keeps students engaged. In addition, it can be helpful to write 2–3 goals for the class session on the board and cross them off as the class progresses. Doing so may provide the student feedback on how productive the class has been. Additional considerations when preparing to organize a class session include: a) What does the instructor want to cover in this class session and approximately how long will be needed to effectively cover the material? b) Can periods of activity be incorporated in between stints of lecture? c) Has the instructor allowed time for questions and/or individual help? More time than expected may be needed to cover certain concepts; therefore, it is recommended that instructors be flexible and yet organized to ensure the information is covered and yet students' needs are being met.

Future Implications

Although lessons about organization may come in unexpected ways, recommendations outlined above may help to thwart or drastically reduce surprise comments on student evaluations of the course regarding instructor planning.

References

Arter, J., & McTighe, J. (2001). Scoring rubrics in the classroom: *Using performance criteria for assessing and improving student performance.* Thousand Oaks, CA: Corwin Press.

Goos, M., & Hughes, C. (2010). An investigation of the confidence levels of course/subject coordinators in undertaking aspects of their assessment responsibilities. *Assessment & Evaluation In Higher Education, 35*(3), 315–324.

Stark, J. S. (2000). Planning introductory college courses: Content, context and form. *Instructional Science, 28*(5), 413–438.

Converting an Adjunct Position to Lecturer or Tenure-Track Position

Linda Christiansen
Indiana University Southeast

Linda Christiansen has taught as an adjunct at four universities within a five-year period, and served as a lecturer for five years (first visiting and then permanent) before moving into a tenure-track position. She is now a full professor of Business, teaching business law, business ethics, and accounting. For the past six years, she has hired, supervised, and mentored the adjunct faculty in Accounting and Business Law.

Keywords: Career Development

Framework

Many adjunct instructors are interested in full-time employment with one university, yet opportunities are limited.

Introduction

After several years of professional employment, I felt a pull to teach at the college level. I contacted all of the schools in the area and was hired to teach on an adjunct basis at three schools — a community college, an undergraduate institution, and a school of law. I later added a fourth school, initially teaching undergraduate courses.

When I began part-time teaching, I did not expect to move to full-time employment. At that time, full-time lecturers were not common and openings for tenure-track positions were rare. Yet I loved academia and desired a career, so I plowed ahead enthusiastically to make myself attractive for academic employment.

You may have heard the expression "You don't dress for the job you have, you dress for the job you want." Take it one step further and think "Don't work the job you have; work the job you want." In the past 20 years, many people have moved from being an adjunct to a full-time lecturer or tenure-track position. The key is to view the situation from the position of your dean or department chair — make his or her job easier and you will be an attractive candidate for hire! As an adjunct, you have the

So I plowed ahead enthusiastically to make myself attractive for academic employment.

• • • • • • • • • • • •

opportunity to be a 'known quantity' for any full-time positions that may open and have a platform to present yourself in what amounts to a very in-depth interview. Make yourself valuable and indispensible.

Teaching—Course Load & Development

The first step to establishing your value to the university entails you accepting any and all requests to teach certain classes. This could include teaching in the hybrid/blended format or fully online, as universities are continuing to add various formats and need willing and capable instructors. As you prove yourself to be able to teach needed classes, the school could become dependent on your skills. Hiring you will add great flexibility for the department in scheduling.

- Uphold standards and maintain quality. Always be prepared. Develop a reputation for being on time and well prepared. Be enthusiastic about your discipline and about teaching. This will inspire students and your colleagues will notice.
- Be devoted to students. While it goes without saying, serving students is the reason we are in the classroom; sometimes, though, that simple reality gets lost in the demands of part-time teaching and other parts of life. Hold office hours and answer emails promptly. Informally encourage and advise students
- Prepare class material in advance. That way, you will not fall victim to a problem with the copier, and you will also be more confident and relaxed before and during class. A frantic rush before class is both upsetting and troublesome. When you are known to be prepared and relaxed, administrators and colleagues will be more likely to continue to hire you and then possibly create a full-time position for you or select you when one becomes available.

Research & Conference Presentation

Research is not required for adjunct positions, nor is it required for most lecturer positions. But, if you are interested in a tenure-track position, having an established track record of research, writing, and presentations adds to your attractiveness. Look for opportunities to partner with faculty who share interests, or where you believe you can add value to research.

An additional benefit of presenting at the conference (or even just attending) is the networking opportunities with faculty from other schools. If there are no openings at your current school, quality conference participation will open up possibilities at other universities.

Service

Like research, service is not required for adjuncts, but it is an avenue to distinguish and make one's self more valuable. Adjuncts may not realize this, but faculty do much of the university administrative work. Any contribution an adjunct can make in that regard frees up full-time employees for other tasks and duties. I found this to be a substantial key to my success in getting the attention of my colleagues and becoming a full-time lecturer and eventually tenure-track. At the very least, most schools need adjunct representation on faculty senate and committees. Ask a faculty member what your service options are.

Relationships with Colleagues

Adjuncts usually visit campus for class only (and perhaps some office hours). Making the effort to meet faculty by attending meetings or campus/school social events will demonstrate your interest and show your value and potential as a full-time instructor.

Professional Development

Most schools allow adjuncts to attending teaching workshops and pedagogical programs. Find the teaching and learning center on campus or ask colleagues about these opportunities. You may even find that you can present at some sessions in areas you have experience or ideas.

Conclusion

The extra investment you do in any area will make your adjunct teaching easier and more effective, as well as potentially lead to a permanent, full-time position. Try some of the ideas included here, and do not hesitate to share your involvement and extra efforts with your dean or department chair. If you establish a reputation of quality, enthusiasm, and preparedness throughout your adjunct teaching, administrators and colleagues will look for opportunities to make you a full-time employee.

The extra investment you do in any area will make your adjunct teaching easier and more effective, as well as potentially lead to a permanent, full-time position.

TEACHING AND LEARNING CENTERS SERVE ALL FACULTY

CHRISTOPHER J. YOUNG
INDIANA UNIVERSITY NORTHWEST

Christopher Young is an assistant professor of History as well as director of the Center for Innovation and Scholarship in Teaching and Learning at IU Northwest. In this role, Christopher works diligently to serve all faculty.

GAIL RATHBUN
INDIANA UNIVERSITY-PURDUE UNIVERSITY FORT WAYNE

Gail Rathbun joined the Center for the Enhancement of Learning and Teaching (CELT) as the director in July 2004 after 4 years at Al Akhawayn University in Ifrane, Morocco. There she helped develop and teach the curriculum for the newly founded Center for Academic Development, and conducted teacher training for AUI and Moulay Ismail University in Meknes.

Keywords: Professional Development, Faculty Development, Learning Technologies, Teaching and Learning Centers

Part-time faculty come from all walks of life and bring to the campus and to the classroom a myriad of experience. In short, part-time faculty colleagues have much to offer to the college and university learning environment.

How a part-time faculty member experiences a campus will likely vary. Whether it is access to office supplies, the copying machine, or office space, each campus has its culture, and the treatment of adjuncts is certainly part of that culture. Though they may often feel as if they are not fully a part of the community in which they labor, adjuncts should know that they are an integral part of the academy. Many full-time faculty have experience working as part-time faculty members, and all academic administrators know their indispensable worth to the functioning of the campus.

Adjunct faculty should seize opportunities for professional development that are available to them as faculty members. Perhaps even as adjuncts receive announcements about professional development opportunities, the perceived reality may be that these workshops are for full-time faculty. This is not so. As directors of the teaching and learning centers on their respective campuses, the authors of this essay want their faculty colleagues who are working on a part-time basis to know that the centers are there to serve them, too. The shared common denominator is responsibility for fostering student learning.

The central mission of teaching and learning centers is to offer professional development opportunities to faculty on each center's respective campus. The staffing resources of each center will often hinge on the size of the campus and its student body. Consequently the number of professional development opportunities may vary significantly from campus to campus. However, while the menu of professional development topics may vary, the goal of each center and the main thrusts of the center's workshops will be remarkably similar whether it is a small or large campus.

Adjunct faculty members are welcome to all teaching and learning center workshops, whether the workshops are face-to-face or virtual. Historically, attendance by adjunct faculty members has been low at these workshops and the staff of the centers recognize the scheduling challenges that our part-time colleagues face. Each center makes an effort to offer professional development opportunities multiple times in order to maximize availability for adjuncts. If you feel that this is not the case on your campus, you are encouraged to make an appointment with the director or associate director of your campus's center for teaching and learning to discuss ways to make workshops more accessible to you. It is important to share this information; if it is happening to you, then it may be happening to your part-time colleagues as well. It would be a rare case for a center not to take your suggestions seriously or to seek some way to accommodate you and others.

In addition to workshops that are open to all faculty on campus, adjunct faculty are encouraged to make individual appointments with teaching and learning staff. Each center will have a staff member that specializes in a particular area such as instructional design or learning technologies. Their job is to consult and serve faculty—all faculty. They would welcome the opportunity to discuss teaching strategies, useful digital applications, course design, or to help you navigate the learning management system employed at your institution. Consultations are available in person within the center or via telephone or email.

Not only are adjunct faculty members encouraged to participate in workshops, take advantage of staff consultants, and apply for development grants sponsored by centers for teaching and learning, but they are also welcome to create, develop, and offer workshops as well. That part-time faculty attendance is low at professional development workshops, and the number of part-time faculty offering their own workshops is even lower may be a symptom of the many demands that are placed on the professional and family lives of adjuncts. It may also be the result of adjuncts not fully realizing that the teaching and learning centers are there to serve them too. The centers are there to provide professional growth as participant or presenter.

A wealth of resources for teaching is available on all teaching center web sites. Many practical tips and tutorials are available online to help the part-time faculty member answer, at any time of day or night, specific questions or learn the particular skills needed. Based on our own experience, we believe that these web-based resources are probably the least used service that teaching centers provide. FACET makes available on its web site a list of links to all teaching centers.

We strongly encourage part-time faculty to visit our teaching and learning center web sites and to drop by the center when on campus. We are committed to helping you be an effective teacher because your success in the classroom is critical to accomplishing the mission of the university.

ANNOTATED BIBLIOGRAPHY

Aldrich, C. (2009). *Learning online with games, simulations and virtual worlds: Strategies for online instruction.* San Francisco, CA: Jossey-Bass.

This book is written by Clark Aldrich who is an educational game consultant. The book provides a rich understanding of the benefits of educational games, a description of games available, and suggestions for when games should be utilized and the preparatory work needed to make them effective in a learning environment.

Ambrose, S. A., Bridges, M. W., DiPietro, M., Lovett, M. C., & Norman, M. K. (2010). *How learning works: Seven research-based principles for smart teaching.* Boston, MA: John Wiley & Sons Inc.

Drawing on principles from cognitive science, the authors illustrate how these principles can be integrated into teaching. The seven chapters cover how prior knowledge affects learning, how organization of knowledge affects learning, the factors that motivate students to learn, how students develop mastery, the kinds of practice and feedback that enhances learning, why student development and course climate matters, and how students become self-directed learners.

Angelo, T. A., & Cross, K. P. (1993). *Classroom assessment techniques: A handbook for college teachers.* San Francisco, CA: Jossey-Bass.

Now a classic book that describes what classroom assessment involves and how to do it successfully. This book provides fifty classroom assessment techniques and step-by-step instructions for using these techniques.

Arter, J. A., & McTighe, J. (2001). *Scoring rubrics in the classroom: Using performance criteria for assessing and improving student performance.* Thousand Oaks, CA: Corwin Press.

Provides a practical approach to assessing creative writing, research projects, and cooperative group activities. Rubrics are defined and the theory behind rubrics is provided. The argument is made that, when used correctly, rubrics allow for the assessment of quality.

Bain, K. (2004). *What the best college teachers do.* Cambridge, MA: Harvard University Press.

Based on a fifteen-year study of almost 100 college teachers, Bain provides his response to the question of what makes a teacher great. He argues that students remember those teachers that communicated that students can learn and that teaching matters.

Barkley, E. F. (2010). *Student engagement techniques: A handbook for all faculty.* San Francisco, CA: Jossey-Bass.

Barkley provides a model for engaging students and over 100 strategies that teachers have found to be effective in engaging students. Each strategy is described with sufficient detail so that others can implement the strategy. Additional resources are also provided.

Bean, J. C. (2011). *Engaging ideas: The professor's guide to integrating writing, critical thinking, and active learning in the classroom (2nd Ed.).* San Francisco, CA: Josey-Bass.

This book is described as a practical nuts-and-bolts guide for teachers from any discipline. Readers are provided ideas for designing writing and critical thinking activities. New information in this edition includes material dealing with genre and discourse community theory, quantitative/scientific literacy, blended learning, and online learning.

Beck, E., & Greive, D. (2008). *Going the distance: A handbook for part-time & adjunct faculty who teach online - Revised first edition.* Ann Arbor, MI: Part-Time Press Inc.

This short book provides general guidance for those new to teaching online. A variety of topics are addressed including: day-to-day challenges, technological preparation, course design, virtual classroom techniques, and virtual field trips.

Berk, R. (2003). *Professors are from Mars, students are from snickers: How to write and deliver humor in the classroom and in professional presentations.* Sterling, VA: Stylus Publishing.

Berk has written several books on the use of humor in teaching. In this book, he provides a rationale, evidence, and helpful hints for those interested in using humor in designing course materials or presentations.

Bligh, D. A. (2000). *What's the use of lectures?* San Francisco, CA: Jossey-Bass.

In the rush to incorporate active learning, lectures are sometimes eliminated or viewed as unimportant. This book provides information about the appropriate (and inappropriate) uses of lectures. Practical suggestions are provided for creating more effective and engaging lectures.

Bloom, B. S. (1984). *Taxonomy of educational objectives: Book 1: Cognitive domain.* London, England: Longman.

Although written almost 40 years ago, this book remains a classic and is widely used. Bloom's taxonomy for classifying skills have been revised but the basic ideas he proposed remain valid.

Blumberg, P. (2013). *Assessing and improving your teaching: Strategies and rubrics for faculty growth and student learning.* San Francisco, CA: Jossey Bass.

Topics included: a teaching model that promotes better learning, a model to assess teaching to promote better learning, self-assessment rubrics, and cases showing effective uses for the rubrics.

Blumberg, P. (2008). *Developing learner-centered teaching: A practical guide for faculty.* Boston, MA: John Wiley & Sons Inc.

This book provides a step-by-step process for moving any teacher-centered course closer to a learner-centered course. The book offers self-assessments and worksheets based on the five practices outlined by Weimer in her book, *Learner-Centered Teaching.*

Boettcher J. V. & Conrad R. (2010). *The online teaching survival guide: Simple and practical pedagogical tips.* San Francisco, CA: Jossey-Bass.

This book provides a theory-based approach to teaching online. Part One of the book focuses on core principles and best practices related to online teaching and learning. Part Two provides what the authors call simple, practical, and pedagogically based tips. Part Three is a single chapter that attempts to provide a look at what might be next in online teaching.

Boice, R. (2000). *Advice for new faculty members: Nihil nimus.* Needham Heights, MA: Allyn and Bacon.

This book advocates for moderation in working as a new faculty member (nothing in excess) based on years of researching faculty who "thrive" versus faculty who did not. A series of practical, easy to follow rules for learning to teach, write, and interact in academia are provided. Rules are focused on maximum gain with the least amount of time and effort.

Bowen, J. A. (2012). *Teaching naked: How moving technology out of your college classroom will improve student learning.* San Francisco, CA: John Wiley & Sons, Inc.

This book presents a compelling case for flipping the classroom. Topics include: the new digital landscape, designing 21st century courses, and strategies for universities of the future.

Bowman, L. (2014). *Online teaching for adjunct faculty: How to manage workload, students, and multiple schools.* Richmond: VA: Amazon Digital Services, Inc.

This book is designed to provide organizational strategies that streamline workload. The premise is that adjunct faculty must work at numerous schools, teaching different classes, creating an unmanageable workload. This book provides strategies and tips to streamline and manage workload, to manage large classes, and to address the unique challenges of dealing with multiple schools.

Brookfield, S. (1995). *Becoming a critically reflective teacher.* San Francisco, CA: Jossey-Bass.

In this book, the author provides four lenses—self, students, colleagues, and theories—through which the teacher can become more critically reflective about his or her teaching. The book provides numerous anecdotes and examples that allow the instructor to explain the author's approach.

Brookfield, S. (2006). *The skillful teacher: On technique, trust and responsiveness in the classroom.* Boston, MA: John Wiley & Sons Inc.

This book provides practical advice about dealing with the many non-content related issues that arise when teaching such as interpersonal issues and potential tensions. The focus of this book is on dealing with the unexpected and the author relies on his experiences as a teacher to provide examples.

Buskist, W. & Benassi, V. (2012). *Effective college and university teaching: Strategies and tactics for the new professoriate.* Los Angeles, CA: Sage Publications.

In this book, a rationale and a detailed guide is provided for effective teaching strategies. The practical, research-based suggestions are useful for improving teaching. The book is aimed at helping graduate students and new faculty become effective teachers but could easily be applied to adjunct faculty and lecturers.

Caulfield, J. (2011). *How to design and teach a hybrid course: Achieving student-centered learning through blended classroom, online and experiential activities.* Sterling, VA: Stylus Publishing.

This book begins with an introductory section that defines hybrid teaching and provided a theoretical underpinning for such courses. Separate chapters address experiential learning and critical questions to consider when engaged in initially planning a hybrid course. Section Two of the book provides greater detail on designing and teaching a hybrid course including using discussion, providing and soliciting student feedback, using small groups, meeting student expectations, and enhancing teaching through the use of technology. The final section summarizes survey data on what students say about hybrid courses, what the best hybrid teachers say about these courses, and what the best hybrid teachers do.

Chism, N. (2007). *Peer review of teaching: A source book (2nd Ed.)*. San Francisco, CA: Jossey-Bass.

This book provides the framework that many across the nation have used to develop their own peer review programs. Chism advocates for the importance of faculty driven peer review with articulate criteria and standards and a systematic review process. This edition includes discussion of peer review in special contexts such as clinics, studios, and practice settings.

Collins, M. (2011). *Teaching in the sciences: A handbook for part-time & adjunct faculty*. Ann Arbor, MI: The Part-Time Press.

This book was designed for use by teaches of any scientific discipline. The author focuses on course development, improving lecture, student retention, teaching non-science majors, written assignments, technology, evaluation, and testing.

Conceicao, S. C. O., & Lehman, R. M. (2011). *Managing online instructor workload: Strategies for finding balance and success*. San Francisco, CA: Jossey-Bass.

This book provides practical strategies, advice, and examples for how to prioritize, balance, and manage an online teaching workload. Part one focuses on issues and challenges when teaching online. Part two focuses on instructors' stories for balancing workload. Part three looks at workload from a design perspective. Part four focuses on managing tasks and prioritizing time. Part five describes using workload strategies for maintaining quality of life. Part six provides final thoughts and practical implications for balancing workload.

Conrad, R., & Donaldson, J.A. (2011). *Engaging the online learner: Activities and resources for creative instruction*. San Francisco, CA: Jossey-Bass.

This book is an updated version of a volume in the Jossey-Bass' Online Teaching & Learning series. The series was designed to help instructors improve online teaching and learning by providing concise, practical resources. The current volume includes updated activities and resources based on changes in technology and best practices.

Cooper, L. E., & Booth, B. A. (2010). *The adjunct faculty handbook*. Thousand Oaks, CA: Sage Publications, Inc.

Topics in this book include: preparing to teach, technology in education, environment of learning, connecting with students, teaching methods, professional development of the adjunct faculty member, evaluation of student performance, and future trends.

Davis, B. G. (2009). *Tools for teaching (2nd Ed.)*. San Francisco: Jossey-Bass.

This resource book is organized into twelve sections: getting started with a course, the changing student body, strategies for discussion, courses with high enrollments, strategies other than lecture or discussion, helping students to become more motivated, enhancing students' writing and problem-solving skills, testing and grading, simple technologies such as PowerPoint, course evaluation, teaching outside the classroom, and end of term issues.

Falk, E. (2012). *Becoming a new instructor: A guide for college adjuncts and graduate students*. New York: Routledge.

Topics included in this book: conceptualizing the class, creating graded assignments, putting together the syllabus, planning in-class time, running your class, grading, interacting with students, and taking your class online.

Filene, P. (2006). *The joy of teaching: A practical guide for new college instructors*. Chapel Hill, NC: Chapel Hill Press.

In this book, the author provides the advantages and disadvantages of various pedagogical strategies, allowing the reader to judge each. Topics include: syllabus writing, lecture planning, class discussions, grading, and teacher-student interactions outside the classroom.

Fink, L. D. (2013). *Creating significant learning experiences: An integrated approach to designing college courses*. San Francisco, CA: Jossey-Bass.

This edition has been significantly updated from the original including new research on how people learn, active learning, online learning, the impact of student engagement on student learning, and the effectiveness of Fink's approach. One of Fink's basic premises is that the key to a quality educational program is creating significant learning experiences.

Gabriel, K. F. (2008). *Teaching unprepared students: Strategies for promoting success and retention in higher education*. Sterling, VA: Stylus Publishing.

This book provides a practical approach to understanding and addressing unprepared students in the classroom while enhancing the classroom experiences for those who are prepared. Doing both is frequently a challenge. Gabriel addresses whether unprepared and at-risk students is a myth or a reality, philosophical foundations, the first week of class, the importance of consistent contact, the science of learning, learner-centered education, assessment, and techniques for promoting academic integrity and discouraging cheating.

Gray, P., & Drew, D. E. (2008). *What they didn't teach you in graduate school: 299 helpful hints for success in your academic career (2nd Ed.)*. Sterling, VA: Stylus Publishing.

Specific, clear advice on a variety of topics appropriate for anyone in academia. Chapter Five of the text specifically focuses on teaching with subsections titled in the classroom, teaching online, and students. Chapter 10, Life as an Academic, provides especially useful advice concerning deans, departmental politics, office hours, freedom of speech, and collegiality. Many topics addressed in this book are rarely seen in a book of this type including: you may become involved in a student grievance, sexual harassment, dealing with student problems, professional travel, protecting your intellectual capital while traveling, diversity, and personal considerations.

Greive, D., & Lesko, P. (2011). *A handbook for adjunct/part-time faculty and teachers of adults (7th Ed.)*. Ann Arbor, MI: The Part-Time Press Inc.

This revised edition includes topics such as: contemporary practices, technology in the classroom, electronic communications, professional ethics, establishing a teaching environment, student-centered learning, characteristics of good teaching, surviving the first class, and teaching/learning styles.

Greive, D. (2006). *Handbook II: Advanced teaching strategies for adjunct and part-time faculty (3rd Ed.)*. Ann Arbor, MI: The Part-Time Press Inc.

This book focuses on realistic approaches to handling difficult situations faced by adjunct and part-time faculty. Topics include: utilizing the techniques of andragogy, the modern student, 101 things you can do the first three weeks of class, developing the environment for learning, connecting with the adult learner, classroom communication, technology in the classroom, critical thinking, the syllabus and lesson plan, motivating students, collaborative/cooperative learning, student learning styles: teaching techniques for the 21st century, teaching students to solve problems, large class teaching tips, diversity, preparing for a distance education assignment, and testing and test strategies.

Greive, D. (2009). *Teaching strategies & techniques for adjunct faculty (5th Ed.)*. Ann Arbor, MI: The Part-Time Press Inc.

Designed for busy professionals, this book is a quick and volume of tips, strategies, and techniques, addressing teaching in the contemporary classroom.

Groccia, J. E., Alsudairi, M. A., & Buskist, W. F. (2012). *Handbook of college and university teaching: A global perspective*. Thousand Oaks, CA: Sage Publications, Inc.

This book begins with a model for understanding university teaching and learning based on research. Material is split into sections on outcomes of teaching and learning, understanding students, understanding teachers, understanding context, understanding content, understanding learning, and understanding teaching.

Hoeller, K. (2014). *Equality for contingent faculty: Overcoming the two-tier system*. Nashville, TN: Vanderbilt University Press.

This book provides a forum for eleven activists from the United States and Canada to describe the problems they see relating to adjunct faculty, share case histories, and offer concrete solutions. The book is split into three parts. The first part describes three accounts of successful organizing efforts within the two-track system. The second part describes how the two-track system divides faculty into haves and have-nots and leaves the majority without the benefit of academic freedom or the support of their institutions. The third part offers roadmaps for overcoming the deficiencies of the two-track system and providing equality for all professors, regardless of status or rank.

Lang, J. (2008). *On course: A week-by-week guide to your first semester of college teaching*. Cambridge, MA: Harvard University Press.

This book literally breaks the semester into fifteen weeks and describes important concepts. The syllabus is provided a chapter 'before the beginning.' Topics include: the first days of class, teaching with technology, lectures, discussions, teaching with small groups, assignments and grading, students as learners, students as people, academic honesty, finding a balance outside the classroom, re-energizing the classroom, common problems, student ratings and evaluations, last days of class, and teachers as people.

Lieberg, C. (2008). *Teaching your first college class: A practical guide for new faculty and graduate student instructors*. Sterling, VA: Stylus.

This book provides tips and the rationale behind these tips. Topics include: on being a novice college teacher, apprehension and trepidations, helping students understand what it means to be educated, pedagogy, teacher-centered or student-centered, critical thinking, active learning, making use of technology, authority in the classroom, diversity, finding out what your students know, constructing a syllabus, grade inflation, student conferences, difficult or challenging topics, humor, what you should know about how well students read, some formats to help jump-start discussions, motivation, planning assignments, writing, group work and presentations, fraud, cheating, plagiarism, grading, and much more.

Lyons, R. E. (2007). *Best practices for supporting adjunct faculty.* Bolton, MA: Anker Publishing Company.

This book focuses on the development of adjunct faculty. Topics include: deepening understanding of adjunct faculty; ensuring an effective start for adjunct faculty; supporting adjunct faculty through face-to-face and online programming; mentoring adjunct instructors in a variety of approaches; building community and a sense of mission; analysis of orientation, pre-service training, recognition, and comprehensive professional development programs for adjunct faculty; portraits of proven programs and strategies for implementing initiatives at your institution; and an adjunct professor's perspective on the benefits of supporting part-timers' teaching.

Lyons, R. E. (2003). *Success strategies for adjunct faculty.* Columbus, OH: Allyn & Bacon.

This book blends research on higher education with practical tools for the adjunct faculty member. The book provides self-analysis tools, course management tools, a model mentoring agreement, an exam development exercise, online support resources, and a chapter on integrating new technology into teaching.

Lyons, R. E., Kysilka, M. L., & Pawlas, G. E. (1998). *The adjunct professor's guide to success: Surviving and thriving in the college classroom.* Needham Heights, MA: Allyn & Bacon.

The book is written for "nonteaching professionals—businesspeople, attorneys, medical professions, and others—who are increasing staffing the largely evening and weekend courses offered by nearly all institutions of higher education" (Lyons, et al. 1998, p. xiii). The book is written as a "how-to" guide for adjunct faculty and is written in an informal style. Topics include "Building Your Part-Time Teaching Career," different learning styles of students and how those should affect classroom presentations, "tips for thriving," bibliographies, numerous check lists and worksheets, sample classroom exercises, , and course syllabi.

Nilson, L. B. (2010). *Teaching at its best: A research-based resource for college instructors (3rd Ed.).* San Francisco, CA: John Wiley & Sons.

Part One, Laying the Groundwork for Student Learning, includes: understanding your students and how they learn, outcomes-centered course design, the complete syllabus, your first day of class, and motivating your students. Part Two, Managing your Courses, includes: copyright guidelines for instructors, preventing and responding to classroom incivility, preserving academic integrity, making the most of office hours, and course coordination between faculty and teaching assistants. Part Three, Choosing and Using the Right Tools for Teaching and Learning, includes: matching teaching methods with learning outcomes, making the lecture a learning experience, leading effective discussions, experiential learning activities, learning in groups, and questioning techniques for discussion and assessment. Part Four, More Tools: Teaching Real-World Problem Solving, includes: inquiry-guided learning, the case method, problem-based learning, quantitative reasoning and problem solving, and problem solving in the sciences. Part Five, Making Learning Easier, includes: getting students to do the readings teaching your students to think and write in your discipline, accommodating different learning styles, using visuals to teach, and using instructional technology wisely. Part Six, Assessing Learning Outcomes, includes: assessing student learning in progress, constructing summative assessments, preparing students for tests, grading summative assessments, and evaluating and documenting teaching effectiveness.

O'Brien, J. G., Millis, B. J., & Cohen, M. W. (2008). *The course syllabus: A learning-centered approach (2nd Ed.).* San Francisco, CA: Jossey-Bass.

This book provides numerous examples illustrating the components of a good syllabus. The book also provides an excellent list of suggested readings on topics related to teaching.

Svinicki, M. D., & McKeachie, W. (2014). *McKeachie's teaching tips: Strategies, research, and theory for college and university teachers (14th Ed.).* Belmont, CA: Wadsworth.

McKeachie has become recognized for his valuable, and common-sense, advice on teaching. This volume is organized into seven parts: getting started, basic skills for facilitating student learning, understanding students, adding to your repertoire of skills and strategies for facilitating active learning, skills for use in other teaching situations, teaching for higher-level goals, and lifelong learning as a teacher.

Wong, O. (2013). *An instructor primer for adjunct and new faculty: Foundations for career success*. Lanham, MD: Rowman & Littlefield Education.

This comprehensive book includes sections titled: welcome to the teaching world of higher education, set the stage before the first day of class, probe into the minds of learning, enter the stage (environment) on the first day of class, tackle the core of teaching—knowledge, unleash the power of the teaching toolbox, navigate through the magic of questioning, integrate with instructional technology, and full-circle accountability.

CONTRIBUTORS

Efua Akoma
Ashford University
Efua.Akoma@ashford.edu

Paul Bates
Griffith University
p.bates@griffith.edu.au

Barbara Beauchamp
Spalding University
bbeauchamp@spalding.edu

Jon Becker
IU Northwest
jbecker@iun.edu

Raymond Benton, Jr.
Loyola University Chicago
rbenton@LUC.edu

Amy E. Bentz
Western Michigan University
amy.e.bentz@wmich.edu

Nichole C. Boutte-Heiniluoma
Ashford University
Nichole.BoutteHeiniluoma@ashford.edu

Mark Bradford
IU South Bend
writer0224@aol.com

Shane R. Brady
University of Oklahoma
srbrady78@gmail.com

Jonathan W. Carrier
Laramie County Community College
jcarrier@lccc.wy.edu

Linda Christiansen
IU Southeast
lchristi@ius.edu

Elizabeth B Connell
Stockton College
elizabeth.connell@stockton.edu

Mary Ange Cooksey
IU East
mcooksey@iue.edu

Beth Dietz-Uhler
Miami University
uhlerbd@miamioh.edu

Marcia Dixson
Indiana Purdue Fort Wayne
dixson@ipfw.edu

Tony Docan-Morgan
University of Wisconsin La Crosse
tdocan@uwlax.edu

Elena Doludenko
IU Bloomington
elendolu@umail.iu.edu

Leslie Elrod
University of Cincinnati
elrodl@UCMAIL.UC.EDU

Mary Embry
IU Bloomington
mcembry@indiana.edu

Diane L. Finley
Prince George's Community College
finleydl@pgcc.edu

Amy Fowkes
Spalding University
afowkes@spalding.edu

Miles Free
Walsh University
MFree@pmpa.org

Jess L. Gregory
Southern Connecticut University
gregoryj2@southernct.edu

Lucy Guevara-Velez
Western Michigan University
lucy.guevara-velez@wmich.edu

Sayonita Ghosh Hajra
University of Georgia
sayonita@uga.edu

Helene Harte
University of Cincinnati
hartehe@ucmail.uc.edu

Ashley Hasty
IU Bloomington
hastya@indiana.edu

Janet E. Hurn
Miami University
hurnje@miamioh.edu

Karen Johnson
karenaka80@yahoo.com

Tarryn Kille
Griffith University
t.kille@griffith.edu.au

Kevin Scott Krahenbuhl
Middle Tennessee State University
kevin.krahenbuhl@mtsu.edu

Angela M. Miller
University of Cincinnati
millai@ucmail.uc.edu

Nathanael G. Mitchell
Spalding University
nmitchell01@spalding.edu

Robin K. Morgan
IU Southeast
rmorgan@ius.edu

Patrick S. Murray
Griffith University
patrick.murray@griffith.edu.au

Mimi O'Malley
Spalding University
momalley@spalding.edu

Kimberly T. Olivares
Indiana University
ktlane@iupui.edu

Mike Polites
IUPUI
mpolites@iupui.edu

Janice Poston
Spalding University
jposton@spalding.edu

Gail Rathbun
IPFW
rathbun@ipfw.edu

Jessie Reed
Spalding University
jreed05@spalding.edu

ShariLynn Robinson-Lynk
University of Michigan
lynshari@umich.edu

Jim Rogers
IU South Bend
rogersji@iusb.edu

Julie Saam
IU Kokomo
jsaam@iuk.edu

Norah C. Slone
Spalding University
norahslone@gmail.com

Zack Thieneman
Spalding University
zack.thieneman@gmail.com

Chantel E. White
IU South Bend
chantel.eliza.white@gmail.com

DeDe Wohlfarth
Spalding University
Dwohlfarth@spalding.edu

Rhonda Wrzenski
IU Southeast
rwrzensk@ius.edu

Christopher Young
IU Northwest
cjy@iun.edu

Jimmy A. Young
California State University, San Marcos
jyoung@csusm.edu

INDEX

CPSIA information can be obtained
at www.ICGtesting.com
Printed in the USA
LVOW03s1617170316
479628LV00005B/12/P